# ANIMADVERSIONS

ON

## THAT PESTILENT HERESY,

# 𝕿𝖍𝖊 𝕾𝖎𝖓𝖋𝖚𝖑𝖓𝖊𝖘𝖘 𝖔𝖋 𝖙𝖍𝖊 𝕳𝖚𝖒𝖆𝖓 𝕹𝖆𝖙𝖚𝖗𝖊

OF

## THE LORD JESUS CHRIST;

AS PROMULGATED BY

## THE REV. EDWARD IRVING, A. M.

IN THE THIRD NUMBER OF THE MORNING WATCH, AND IN HIS ORTHODOX
AND CATHOLIC DOCTRINE OF OUR LORD'S HUMAN NATURE.

## IN A LETTER

TO A HIGHLY HONOURABLE INDIVIDUAL.

𝖂𝖎𝖙𝖍 𝕹𝖔𝖙𝖊𝖘.

---

## By W. H. COLYER.

---

" Ah, it is a fearful Siege which is at present carrying on against the very Citadel of GOD's own Holy Being, and Man's free Inheritance in His Grace; and WE, who should have been as one man to defend GOD's Holy Being, and our own goodly Inheritance in His Grace, are like the Sons of *Ephraim drunken*, but *not* with *strong drink*, DRUNKEN WITH DELUSION, AND THE CUP OF ERROR !" MR. IRVING'S *Orthodox Doctrine*, 155.

" Now the SPIRIT speaketh expressly, that in the latter times some shall depart from the Faith, giving heed to seducing Spirits, and Doctrines of *Devils*." 1 *Tim.* iv. 1.

" There must be also Heresies among you, that they who are approved may be made manifest." 1 *Cor.* ii. 19.

" *Nevertheless*, the *Foundation* of GOD standeth *sure*; having this *Seal—The LORD knoweth them that are His*." 2 *Tim.* ii. 19.

---

𝕻𝖚𝖇𝖑𝖎𝖘𝖍𝖊𝖉 𝖇𝖞 𝕽𝖊𝖖𝖚𝖊𝖘𝖙.

SOLD BY WESTLEY AND DAVIS, STATIONERS' COURT.

LONDON.

## ERRATA.

Pa. 27. line 19. read, in spite *of* unholy Creation.

    38. ... 14. .... " a Tree to be *desired* to make wise."

    51. ... 17. .... *that* his Christ was not a Sinner.

    66. ... 28. .... really makes it, *or* proves it.

    70. ... 33. .... that desperate*ly* wicked Manhood.

    77. ... 21. omit, *laid*, in *Isa.* liii. 6.

PRINTED BY E. JUSTINS & SON, BRICK LANE, SPITALFIELDS.

# PREFACE.

———

THE following Letter, with some small alterations, was written twelve months ago to a highly honourable Individual who had requested the Author's sentiments on the subject of which it treats. A Copy having found its way into the hands of several venerable and highly respectable Ministers and Members of the Church of CHRIST, who strongly urged its publication — and certain other circumstances, of far greater weight with the Author than any solicitation or recommendation even from Christian Men or from Christian Ministers, however venerable or deservedly beloved in the Church of GOD, having subsequently determined him to " Publish," and to " Conceal not," his sentiments thus privately expressed—a few copies would have issued from the Press during the last summer, had not the Author just then seen, for the first time, a Second Edition, in a very enlarged form, of the Original Essay that had given rise to his epistolary Remarks ; the perusal of which induced him to defer the publication of his Letter until he had replied to some of the most material parts introduced into such new edition, by adding the Notes that are now subjoined.    On that account, in part, and partly through frequent Indisposition, and some other hindrances unnecessary to be particularized here, so much delay has taken place in the appearance of the Letter—which still retains the title of " Observations," &c. prefixed to the Copy above referred to —while the addition of the Notes has induced the Author to send forth the whole as his " Animadversions on that Pestilent Heresy, the Sinfulness of the Human Nature of the Lord Jesus Christ."

The Reader will therefore bear in mind the distinct occasions of the subsequent pages : the *Letter* being a Reply to an Essay from the pen of " *The* Rev. *Edward Irving*, A. M. Minister of the *Scotch* Church, Regent Square, *London*," which appeared in No. III. of *The Morning Watch,* under the Title of "The *true* Humanity of Christ;"—and the *Notes* being the Author's Remarks on the additional matter contained in an enlarged edition of such Essay, which was published by *Mr. Irving* in the beginning of the present year, under the Title of " The Orthodox and Catholic Doctrine of our Lord's Human Nature.'' The Letter should therefore be read first *without* the Notes, and then *with* them ; otherwise the unusual length of some of them, occasioned by the numerous quotations and references given, might destroy that remembrance of the connexion in the Letter which it is desirable should be retained.

"It is a pestilent Heresy," *Mr. Irving* declares of the Sentiment he opposes in his *Orthodox Doctrine,* "which, coming in," he says, " will root out Atonement, Redemption, Regeneration, the Work of the Spirit, and the Human Nature of Christ altogether !'' " It is a pestilent Heresy," I reply, concerning that very Doctrine *Mr. Irving* maintains— the inherent *Sinfulness* of the Humanity of Jesus—" which, coming in, will not only root out the Atonement, Redemption, Regeneration, the Work of the Spirit, and the Human Nature of Christ altogether," but will also " destroy Revelation in the Mass"—annihilate "the great Mystery of Godliness, God manifest in the Flesh"—and exterminate the very existence of the Godhead itself! Since *Mr. Irving* avows, that, what the Scriptures of Truth declare was " *That* Holy Thing," (which was begotten of the Holy Ghost and born of the Virgin *Mary,*) was " *Sinful Substance*"—a *Mass* of *Iniquity*"—&c. And thus he sets aside God's Testimony in order to establish *his own !* He also maintains that Christ had *two Godheads:* the one, he terms " His ABSOLUTE *Godhead"*—and the other, " His LIMITED *Godhead."* This *absolute Godhead* he also calls " the *Person* of the SON OF GOD ;" to which he pretends the *limited* Godhead, " before all worlds," was united; and then His "SINFUL *Manhood"* became united to *that!* And thus, by the intervention of this monstrous Notion of a " *limited"* *Godhead*, (which is, of course, a *second,* and an *inferior* one ; and which *Mr. Irving* brings forth in order to reconcile to carnal Reason the " great Mystery of Godliness,") he doth, in effect, *destroy* the *Mystery,* and deny the immediate Union of the *Human* Nature with the *Divine* in the Person of CHRIST, by the introduction of such *limited Godhead* as a *Link* between the " *absolute Godhead"* and " *sinful Manhood;"*—as may be seen more at large in some of the Notes to the following Pages. And to shew how *Mr. Irving's* Notions would even *exterminate* the very GODHEAD itself, I observe, that he makes the GODHEAD of the FATHER to have been *emptied out* of *Itself* upon the SON—the GODHEAD of the SON to become *contractible* and *contracted*—and the " INFINITE GODHEAD" to have been *conveyed* by the HOLY GHOST *into* the *Person* of the SON ! And thus, having made the Son even *trebly Divine,* and at the expense of the *self-existence* of the FATHER and of the HOLY GHOST, *Mr. Irving* at last makes *his Christ* " INSTEAD of being the SON OF GOD, to become the Son of Man"—to have *emptied Himself* of His " *absolute Godhead,"* or "*Godhead Properties"*—and then to have assumed the *inferior* or " *limited Godhead,"* in order to appear in that " Sinful Substance," that " Mass of Iniquity," as he is pleased to call the inherently Holy Humanity of GOD's HOLY CHILD JESUS.*

Now, believing beyond a doubt that *Mr. Irving's* Sentiment of the *inherent Sinfulness* of the Human Nature of the LORD JESUS CHRIST is not only a grievous Error, " a destructive Falsehood, which by the ingenuity of *Satan,* and the perversity of Men, is fabricated out of precious Truth"—

---

* See the *Notes* on pp. 23, 31, 38.

but that his *whole System* is a System of Error—a *Counter-feit Christianity*—an awful *Delusion,* " which cannot be held, nor favoured, nor borne with, save at the greatest risk and peril to immortal Souls"—the Author of these pages were a most unworthy and unfaithful Witness to that measure of the gift of the knowledge of CHRIST, which the LORD in His Mercy may have bestowed upon him, if he did not deliver his *own* Soul by a plain and fearless Testimony to "the Truth as it is in JESUS;" regardless alike of the smiles or of the frowns of the children of Men.

" It is required in Stewards that a man be found faithful; and as *Mr. Irving* considers *himself* justified in plainly declaring what he believes to be true, and has denounced the *inherent* HOLINESS of Christ's Human Nature as a " Strong Delusion"—an " Heretical Doctrine," &c. and those who hold it as " given up of GOD to believe a Lie ;" and declares of all such Persons, that they are to him as Heathen Men and Publicans ; and as he doth so nauseate and repudiate the *true* Doctrine of the inherent *Holiness* of the LORD JESUS, as contained in the Holy Scriptures ; and doth avow his entire rejection of it, in language which would for ever deprive himself of all Hope were GOD to take him at his own words; and as *Mr. Irving* thinks *himself* perfectly justified in attacking with " unsparing destructiveness," what *he* is pleased to consider " the present fabric of Ignorance and Error"—the Author of these pages considers himself also as fully justified in answering *Mr. Irving* with equal plainness and faithfulness, and as much as possible in his own words, or in the words of Holy Scripture. For, whether men will hear, or whether they will forbear—whether they may approve of his faithfulness, or denounce it as uncharitableness—it behoves him to " Cry aloud and spare not : to lift up his voice like a Trumpet," against the Abominations *Mr. Irving* would bring into the Church as the great Truths of GOD ; being fully assured, as he is, that the Errors *Mr. Irving* has advanced have not the smallest vestige of either Charity or Mercy for any convinced Sinner who feels himself " ready to perish ;"

nor can they afford the smallest ground of *real* Faith and Hope to any Soul of Man who has ever been "taught of the Lord" to see an "end of all Perfection, knowing His Commandment to be exceeding broad." For, what "*Faith* of the Operation of GOD" can any truly convinced Sinner have in a *Christ not revealed* in the Word of GOD—in *Mr. Irving's* Inherently *Sinful* SAVIOUR? Or what scriptural *Hope* in a *Justification* from all Transgression, by one, who, according to *his* account, has rendered no Satisfaction to the punitive Justice of the offended Lawgiver? Or what reliance in any *Sanctification*, in and through an Object whose very *Nature* is declared to have had inherent in it every variety of *Human Wickedness?* Or what confidence in an *Atonement* for the Soul, without *Reconciliation* to GOD by the Blood of the holy, harmless, undefiled Lamb of GOD? in whom there *never* was any inherent *Wickedness*, but who *ever* possessed inherent *Holiness?* " The Prophet that *hath* a *Dream* let *him* tell a Dream; and he that *hath* MY WORD, let him *speak* MY Word *faithfully*. For what is the *Chaff* to the *Wheat*, saith the LORD?"

The Doctrine opposed in the subsequent pages, is not a matter of *minor* moment; a mere difference in Human Opinion concerning some external Observance, in which both parties may be *partially right* without either being *ruinously wrong;* but it is that which involves the most momentous consequences to the present and everlasting welfare of the Souls and Bodies of Men—namely, the *Inherent Sinfulness* of the *whole Human Nature* of the LORD JESUS CHRIST, from his miraculous Conception in the Virgin until His Resurrection from the Tomb; and which is, in fact, the very Life and Soul of *Mr. Irving's* System. Take away *that*, and the *whole* of his " Orthodox and Catholic Doctrine of our Lord's Human Nature" falls to the ground; he himself having declared that, " if *this* PRINCIPLE *must go to the Wall*, HE *must go to the Wall along with it?"\** And this is evident

***

\* *Ortho. Doc.* p. 128—p. 23.—*The Times* of 14th Oct. 1830.

enough when we consider also, that every Doctrine of his is " founded upon it ; that his own Faith and Hope centre in it ; and every thing in *his* Christianity is, more or less, inseparably connected with it ;" and that, of every Individual who *opposes* it, he declares, that " God has sent *that* Man strong Delusion, that he should believe a Lie !" and that he himself " will sooner *die* than relinquish one Iota of it."   And yet, with marvellous inconsistency, *Mr. Irving* has since publicly *denied* that he holds that Christ's Human Nature was *sinful !* His Letter to the Editor of *The Times* Newspaper of the 14th of *October* last, has avowed, that, on the contrary, " he holds with all Orthodox Men that it was " *without Sin*," by the anointing of the Holy Ghost !" In this way *Mr. Irving denies,* in one place, what, in another, he assures us he *believes.* And as he declares in his " Orthodox Doctrine," that the inherent *sinfulness* of Christ's Human Nature is " The *Foundation* of the Orthodox Faith," and " the *only one Faith* of the Church," (which in the above-mentioned Letter to " *The Times*" he evidently contradicts,) who is to know *what* he really *does* believe, after so *public* a *denial* of his *own Faith,* and of what he declares to be " the *only one* Faith of the *Church,* and the uniform Testimony of the *Scriptures* of *Truth ?*"

Many Persons who read with great attention *Mr. Irving's* Letter in " *The Times,*" naturally concluded that he had *renounced* the Doctrine which he previously maintained, of the " inherent Sinfulness of the Human Nature of the Lord Jesus Christ ;" because he so expressly declared therein, that, on the *contrary* (or, as his very words are, " *whereas*) he held with all *Orthodox* men, that it was without sin, by the anointing of the Holy Ghost." . And yet, the truth is, that *Mr. Irving* has not *renounced* one *jot* or *tittle* of all that he has asserted in his " Orthodox and Catholic Doctrine," concerning the inherent Sinfulness and desperate Wickedness of the Humanity of Jesus ; but that he still secretly maintains the same, however he may sometimes find it convenient not to *avow* it, and at others even to *cloak* it, under terms which do not set forth his *own* views, but which exhibit those of his Opponents! For instance, he will profess, that "the eternal SON OF GOD did take upon Him *Man's Nature* with all the *essential Properties* and *common Infirmities* thereof, "yet *without Sin*." Now, by the term "common Infirmities," all the advocates for the inherent *Holiness* of CHRIST's Human Nature include hungering, thirsting, weeping, &c. but *Mr. Irving*, by the use of such terms, means to include also every one of those "*sinful Propensities*" and "inherent *Inclinations to evil*," that ever were possessed by *fallen Human Nature* in its very worst state: asserting as he does, that "Manhood after the Fall broke out into Sins of every name and aggravation; corrupt to the very Heart's Core, and from the centre of its inmost Will, sending out Streams black as Hell." That "*this* is the Human Nature which *every man* is clothed upon withal, which the SON OF MAN was clothed upon withal, bristling thick and strong with Sin like the hairs upon the Porcupine!!!"*—That, "in such a Flesh (*i. e.* as all other men's,) *loving* the *Temptation* and ever *conversing* with the *Tempter*," *Mr. Irving* asserts, the "*Athanasian* Creed doth declare that CHRIST subsisted!"—Whereas it is *Mr. Irving himself* who makes such an awful Declaration, and then lays it to the charge of *Athanasius!* Much as there may be of the "subtlety of the Serpent" in all this, I fear we shall find no traces of the "harmlessness of the Dove." And until *Mr. Irving* shall refer us to the volume, and to the page, wherein *Athanasius* has made the above assertion, every honest enquirer after Truth who reads the above quotation, may justly suspect *Mr. Irving* of dishonesty in Interpretation, or of handling the words of an Author deceitfully, in order to serve his own sinful System; and all such might well address him in the very language of Holy Writ; "Let him bring forth his witnesses, that he may be justified, or let him hear and say, It is Truth."

How then, it may be asked, can *Mr. Irving* assert with one breath, that CHRIST's Human Nature was *inherently*

* *Ortho. Doc.* p. 126.

*Sinful;* and with the next, that He was *perfectly Holy?* On a careful inspection of his statements, we shall find, that he thinks he has accomplished this by having recourse to these two expedients :—the *first* of which is, by making CHRIST'S *Divine* Nature *only* to constitute His *Person,* (and hence His *Human* Nature *Mr. Irving* thinks he may charge with having inherent in it " every variety of Human Wickedness" without in any degree implicating the *Person* of CHRIST with Sin," such Humanity being called by him a " *Nature,*" and not a part of Christ's Person)—And the *second* is, by making the *Power* of the HOLY GHOST to act in, or upon, the inherently sinful *Manhood* of CHRIST, not so as to *change* it in any way from Sinfulness into Holiness, but merely, by Almighty Energy, to RE*strain* its still inherently sinful Propensities from the outward commission of those evils to which both his Body and Soul were inherently *inclined;* and to CON*strain* them, by the same Almighty Power, to the performance of those things which are good, and to which His Sinful Body and Soul must have been naturally *averse.* On these two Delusions—namely, that the *Person* of CHRIST was His *Divine* Nature *only,* and that *his Christ* with a *Sinful* Human Nature was nevertheless to be called *holy—* *Mr. Irving* thinks he may assert whatever his " unsober Fancy" may dictate to his " unbridled Spirit," concerning the inherent Sinfulness and desperate Wickedness of His Manhood, without implicating, in the smallest possible degree, the *Person* of *his Christ* with Sin ; because *he* says it is the *Person* that sinneth, and not the *Nature* which CHRIST'S *Person* took ; and as he makes Christ's Person to consist of His GODHEAD *only,* therefore *he pretends,* that CHRIST could not be chargeable with *any* SIN, nor with *any* UNHOLINESS, although he had " EVERY VARIETY of *Human Wickedness* INHERENT in His *Human Nature*" from His Conception until His Resurrection ! A faithful exposure of either of these two Delusions, lays the Axe to the very Roots of *Mr. Irving's* System of the inherent Sinfulness of CHRIST ; and, against *both,* the following pages wage an incessant war ;

with weapons that are not carnal, but "mighty through GOD to the pulling down of strong holds." The reader must therefore expect to hear of such exposures again and again; "line upon line, and line upon line; here a little, and there a little; here a little, and there a little," and in very plain terms, from the commencement even unto the conclusion, both of the Letter and of the Notes; because *Mr. Irving* has but every where interwoven those Errors in the statements made in his Publication; and, not unfrequently, with so much subtlety in his mode of expression, that they would not be immediately detected by a mere cursory observer. For instance: he will express the first-mentioned Error, thus—that CHRIST was ONE *Person* IN *two* NATURES;" and then assert that " he would not give the Truth expressed in these words of the Catechism, ' *two* distinct *Natures* and ONE *Person* for ever,' for all the Truths that by Human Language have ever been expressed." Under these descriptions of " One Person *in* two Natures," and " two distinct Natures *and* One Person," *Mr. Irving* will still hold that the *Divine* Nature *only* was the *Person* of CHRIST; and that the *Human* Nature was *inherently Sinful*. For, it should be observed, that in the above words he does not assert, as the Truth is, (and as he would have asserted had he *really* held the Truth,) that CHRIST was a *complex* Person OF two Natures—the Human being in Union *with* the Divine, and as much a part of the *Person* of CHRIST *as* the Divine—but he says that CHRIST's *Person* was " IN two Natures." *Mr. Irving's* Statements therefore do not maintain the Truth, that CHRIST's *Person* was *complex*, but that it was *simple*—being Divine *only*—although he will hold that such Divine Person was *in* the *Human* Nature, yet that the *Human* Nature was no part *of* His *Person;* since that would destroy his System at once, because he knows that the moment he admits that the Sinful Human Nature of *his Christ* really formed a part of His *Person*, that very moment his own premises make *his Christ* to be a Sinner; and bring even *Mr. Irving* himself under that awful sentence of condemnation which his own pen has pronounced against all those who so do; namely, of being "worthy to die the death of all Blasphemers, to be stoned by the multitude in the open face of day." So exceedingly great is that *Darkness* which by some men is called *Light*, that, under its influence, they condemn themselves in the very things that they allow; and unconsciously pass the most awful sentence on themselves, in those very Anathemas they thus pronounce against others.

The readiness with which *Mr. Irving* sometimes covers his erroneous Sentiments under "a form of sound Words" from the Church of which he is a Minister, makes such Doctrines the more baneful to the weak in Faith; just as the Counterfeit becomes more extensively injurious, in proportion to the greater value of the Sterling Coin that is imitated, and the nicety of the external resemblance between the false and the true. And still more injurious does *Mr. Irving's* Doctrine appear, when he perverts even the written Word of GOD in order to support his Errors; by asserting, as he does, that every passage of Scripture which declares CHRIST to have come in the *Flesh*, which declareth THE WORD to be made *Flesh*, which declareth GOD to be manifested in the *Flesh*, is a *proof* total and complete that He came in *Sinful* Flesh!" In this way *Mr. Irving* may be said "to hold the Truth in Unrighteousness!" Not indeed in unrighteousness of *Life*, but certainly in unrighteousness of *Interpretation:* wresting as he does, even the very "Scriptures of Truth" to the exhibition of a *False Christ*, which none of his Father's knew; and to the propagation of "another Gospel" than that which the Apostles preached, which is yet *not another*, but a *perversion* of the Gospel—and which *perversion* he nevertheless avows to be the "*Orthodox* Doctrine of the Church of *Scotland!*"

*Mr. Irving* deplores, in very feeling terms, the cold and lifeless condition into which he informs us his own Church has fallen; and from which he would fain restore her, by setting forth, as he tells us he has done, the *faithful* Interpretation of the *Creed* of that Church, in the Sentiments he has avowed in his " Orthodox and Catholic Doctrine of our LORD's Human Nature." *If* this be *true*, then the Church of *Scotland* certainly owes to *Mr. Irving*, in a very pre-eminent degree, a lasting debt of gratitude for being " faithful amongst so many faithless found ;" and for having given us, " in these most ignorant days," the " ancient foundations" of his Mother Church. But, *if* this be *false*—and the Church of *Scotland* does *not* hold the *Sinfulness*, the *Inherent Sinfulness* of the Humanity of the LORD JESUS, surely that Church owes a duty to *herself* to defend her *real* sentiments against such awful Corruptions and ruinous Interpretations of them—whoever may be the false Interpreters, and however they may propagate their destructive Interpretations.

*Mr. Irving* has been calling long enough, and loud enough, one would have thought, to have roused any *healthy* Body to some energetic measures in defence of its own existence ; but since he assures us that the Church of *Scotland* is a *very lethargic* Body, we need not wonder that, by the publication of his Soul-destroying Errors, he should have thundered (even at the very portal of the Church of which he boasts himself an *Orthodox* Minister,) so long, so loud, in vain,

" AWAKE! ARISE! or *be* for ever *fallen !*"*

---

* Some measures have at length been taken by the Presbytery of the *Scotch* Church in *London*, in consequence of *Mr. Irving's* " Orthodox and Catholic Doctrine of our Lord's Human Nature," which he seems to have apprehended, if we may judge by what he says on the 120th page; " The Church of *Scotland* is awaking ; her chains of sleep are breaking : O GOD! may it not be to destroy those her Sons who have aroused her out of the sleep of death, in which she might have lain till the voice of the Archangel and the Trump of GOD." Of this Church, (which he here represents as " just awaking from the sleep of Death," by mere effect of *human* agency,) it has long been *Mr. Irving's* boast that he was both a Member and a Minister ; as it has of late become his glorying that he ranks amongst the most *Orthodox* Divines of that Church; in which he makes the grand Test of Orthodoxy to consist, in holding that " Pestilent Heresy," the Inherent Sinfulness of the Human Nature of the LORD JESUS: (which *Mr. Irving* professes to have believed even " from his Childhood," with an unwavering faith, pa 67.) It may now be asked, however, whether *Mr. Irving* really continues a *Member* of the Church of *Scotland* or not? If he

The Author of the following pages cannot discharge his own conscience in closing these prefatory remarks, without plainly declaring his firm belief, that *all Mr. Irving's* ERRORS originate in his *not knowing* the Scriptures by the *teaching* of the SPIRIT of GOD : confessing, as *Mr. Irving* does, in the very opening of his " Orthodox and Catholic Doctrine of our Lord's Human Nature," that " it is of the *Essence* of the *Truth*, that it is *all* that the *Truth* is *worth*, to maintain that *Regeneration*, or Impartation of the HOLY GHOST, *addeth* nothing, *withdraweth* nothing, *changeth* nothing of our created substance, but by an invisible *Person* of GODHEAD

---

does—will that Church allow him to remain within her pale as an acknowledged *faithful* Interpreter of her Creed ? or will she publicly disown him in the face of all his veneration for her Antiquity, and superior Orthodoxy ?    But if *Mr. Irving* does *not* now continue a Member of that Church, why does he not openly avow his Separation from her ?    Heterodox as she must now appear to him to be, either in her *Creed*, or in her Ministers' *Interpretation* of it !

Since the *London* Presbytery have given *publicity* to their disapprobation of *Mr. Irving's* Errors, as proclaimed by him to the World, it seems that some more *private* mode of dealing with a *public* Offence, would have been more agreeable to the Offender.    But the Apostle's direction is, that those who *offend* before *all*, should be *rebuked* before *all*, " that others might also fear ;" (1 *Tim.* v. 20.) and this was the Apostle's practice too, when he withstood *Peter* " before all," because *before all* he was to be blamed, *Gal.* ii. 14.    *Mr. Irving* will never surely presume to say, that his Errors have been promulgated " in a corner," however he may sometimes seek to shun their public Examination and Condemnation ; and at other times appear to *cloak*, if not most studiously to *avoid* them.

Of such Concealment of his real Sentiments, the following " Declaration," so recently made known in the Public Prints, may be given in evidence, in addition to that other Public Document before referred to, *Mr. Irving's* Letter to the Editor of *The Times*, of the 14th of October last :—

" DECLARATION *of the* SESSION *of the* NATIONAL SCOTCH CHURCH.

*London, 15th Dec.* 1830.

" We, the Minister, Missionary, Elders, and Deacons of the National " *Scotch* Church, Regent Square, feel it a duty we owe to ourselves, to the " Congregation to which we belong, to the Church of CHRIST, and to all " honest men, no longer to remain silent under the heavy charges that are " brought against us, whether from Ignorance, Misapprehension, or wilful " Perversion of the Truth ; and therefore we solemnly declare—

controlleth and overcometh it," (pp. 4, 5.) In which assertions *Mr. Irving* not only confounds things that essentially differ—namely, the Divine *Act* of the HOLY GHOST in Regeneration with the Divine *In-dwelling* of the Almighty Regenerator in the Soul regenerated by His Power—(since he speaks of Regeneration and the Inhabitation of the HOLY GHOST as One and the same thing,) but he virtually denies there is any *real* REgeneration at all; by stating, as he does, that *in* Regeneration there is no *addition* to, no *withdrawment* from, nor any *change* of, the Person regenerated; but that "an invisible *Person* of GODHEAD *controls* and *overcomes*"

---

" That we utterly detest and abhor any Doctrine that would charge with
" Sin, original or actual, our blessed LORD and SAVIOUR JESUS CHRIST,
" whom we worship and adore as " the very and Eternal GOD : of one Sub-
" stance, and equal with the FATHER; who, when the fulness of the Time
" was come, did take upon Him man's nature, with all the essential Proper-
" ties and common Infirmities thereof, yet without Sin"—" very GOD and very
" Man, yet one CHRIST, the only Mediator between GOD and Man"—who, in
" the days of His Flesh was "holy, harmless, undefiled, and full of Grace and
" Truth"—"who through the ETERNAL SPIRIT offered Himself without Spot
" to GOD"—" the LAMB of GOD that taketh away the Sin of the World"—
" a Lamb without Blemish and without Spot"—in which offering of Him-
" self, " He made a proper, real, and full Satisfaction to his FATHER's Jus-
" tice in our behalf."    And we further declare, that all our Peace of
" Conscience, progress in Sanctification, and Hope of eternal Blessedness,
" resteth upon the Sinlessness of that Sacrifice, and the Completeness of that
" Atonement which he hath made for us as our Substitute.

" And finally we do solemnly declare, that these are the Doctrines which
" are constantly taught in this Church, agreeably to the Standards of the
" Church of *Scotland*, and the Word of GOD."

EDWARD IRVING, *Minister.*

DAVID BROWN, *Missionary.*

| | | |
|---|---|---|
| ARCHIBALD HORN. | | CHARLES VERTUE. |
| DAVID BLYTH. | | ALEX. GILLESPIE, Jun. |
| WM. HAMILTON. | | JOHN THOMSON. |
| DUNCAN MACKENZIE. | | J. C. HENDERSON. |
| JA. NISBET. | *Elders.* | THOS. CARSWELL. |
| | | DAVID KER.      *Deacons.* |

From " THE WORLD," *Monday, Dec.* 20, 1830.

the Man; who, in himself, is just the same "*natural* Man"
*after Mr. Irving's* pretended REgeneration has taken place,
as he was *before*. What then is, in fact, RE-*generated*, according to *Mr. Irving's* unscriptural statement of the Doctrine ?
Or what is that which *feels* Sin—*hates* Sin—*confesses* Sin—
*mourns* on account of Sin—*cries* to GOD for the pardon of Sin,
and for deliverance from it, in all those who are *truly* regenerated of the HOLY GHOST, or are *really* "born of God ?" The
MAN *himself, Mr. Irving* makes to remain the very same unchanged, natural, or carnal creature he was before his pretended
regeneration ; and it is most evident that none of the above

---

That the above "solemn Declaration" should have deceived many persons,
and that they should have supposed *Mr. Irving* had renounced "that most
fearful Error," which he has made the very soul or spirit of His "Orthodox
Doctrine"—namely, the Inherent Sinfulness of our LORD's Human Nature—
is not to be wondered at when we find him cloaking so deadly a Heresy under
those very terms that express his *Opponents'* views but *not* his *own !* Here I
refer more immediately to his saying, that he believes, that "when the fulness
of the time was come (the LORD JESUS CHRIST) did take upon him Man's Nature, with all the essential Properties and common Infirmities thereof, *yet* WITH-
OUT SIN." Now it cannot be "from Ignorance, Misapprehension, or from
Wilful Perversion of the Truth," as *Mr. Irving* would have us to believe, that
"such heavy charges are brought against him" of maintaining the Inherent
Sinfulness of the whole Human Nature which our LORD took, when we
refer to his own Statements, that "Manhood after the Fall broke out into Sins
of every name and aggravation ; corrupt to the very Heart's Core, and from the
centre of its inmost Will sending out Streams black as Hell. *This* is the Human Nature which every man is clothed upon withal, *which the* SON OF MAN
*was clothed upon withal, bristling thick and strong with Sin like the Hairs upon
the Porcupine.*" (*Ortho. Doc.* p. 126.) That "in such a reasonable Soul (as all
other men's) liable to Temptation through the Flesh, and in such a Flesh *loving*
the *Temptation*, and *ever conversing with* the TEMPTER, (*Mr. Irving* asserts that
"the *Athanasian Creed* declares," when it is himself only who makes the assertion) that CHRIST subsisted"—(pa. 37.) And that "if any Man will say, that
CHRIST's Flesh was not Sinful Flesh, as ours is, with the same Dispositions,
and Propensities, and Wants, and Afflictions, then I say, (*Mr. Irving* adds) GOD
hath sent *that* man strong Delusion, that he should believe a Lie." (pa. 23.)

Why, then, does *Mr. Irving* altogether *avoid*, in the above "Solemn
Declaration" of the Doctrines preached by him, a plain and honest Statement of
that *one* in particular, which he has declared to be the very *Basis* of the Christian
Faith, in his "Orthodox and Catholic Doctrine?" even the inherent Sinfulness of

Acts of the *truly* regenerated character, such as contrition, and confession on account of Sin, &c. can be at all applicable to that " invisible *Person* of GODHEAD" who is made by *Mr. Irving* to inhabit his *unchanged Natural Man!* Surely that very weighty Interrogatory of our LORD to *Nicodemus*, might well be addressed to *Mr. Irving* also, in reference to the very same subject : " Art THOU a MASTER of *Israel*, and knowest not *these* things ?" It is evident that a Man cannot receive one *feeling* of a *Life* which he does not possess. And as all men by nature are destitute of any *spiritual* Life, being all " dead in trespasses and in sins," if

---

the Humanity of JESUS, from his Conception in the Virgin until His Resurrection from the Tomb ? He tells us, in his " Solemn Declaration," that he believes the SON of GOD " took upon Him Man's Nature, with all the essential Properties and common Infirmities thereof," *yet* " WITHOUT *Sin.*" Whereas, in his " Orthodox and Catholic Doctrine" he assures us, that He took Man's Nature " with all the *evil Propensities* of the *fallen Manhood.*"—(64.) " Sinful Flesh as ours is."—(23.) " Very Flesh of Sin."—(12.) " Flesh of that Kind and Property which betrayeth and tempteth all other persons unto Sin."—(20.) A Body and Soul that were " obnoxious and inclined unto Evil."—(7.) That " His Flesh did carry up to Him every form of Seduction."—(25.) And, that " if a thing must be named by those *Properties,* which it ever hath in itself, and not from those which it derives from another thing most widely different and distinct from itself, then must CHRIST's Flesh be called *Sin*-FUL, and NOT *Sin*-LESS."—(20.) " Flesh ever loving the Temptation, and ever conversing with the Tempter."—(37.) " His Human Nature differed nothing from ours, in its alienation and guiltiness."—(88.) " Our fallen Nature, with all its natural and inherent Propensities."—" The nature of the apostate sinful Creature."—(88.) " The *very Substance* which *fell* in *Adam,* and which hath brought all mankind into *Sin* and Misery."—(108.) " It being *most Orthodox,* (he says, pa. 127.) and of the *Substance* and *Essence* of the Orthodox Faith, to hold that CHRIST could say until His Resurrection, *Not I,* but *Sin* that *tempteth* ME in My Flesh ; just as after His Resurrection He could say, " I am separate from Sinners." And, moreover, he believes, " that the only difference between His Body of Humiliation and His Body of Resurrection is in this very thing, that Sin inhered in the Human Nature, making it mortal and corruptible, till that very time that He rose from the dead : *and if* THIS *Principle must go to the wall, He shall go to the wall along with it!*"—(127, 128.)

Why, then, I ask, has not *Mr. Irving* plainly and honestly avowed, in his " Solemn Declaration," that he still holds that CHRIST took our " *Sinful*

there be *no real Change* that passes on the regenerate, (and *Mr. Irving* affirms there is *none*) it is equally evident that all such Persons, though *called regenerate by Mr. Irving*, are absolute *un*regenerate ; and are just as " dead in trespasses and in sins" as are any of the finally reprobate.

This supposed Regeneration without *change,* seems to have been invented by *Mr. Irving,* in order that, either by comparison, or by inference, or by both, he might have some plausible pretence for saying, as he does, that there was no more inherent Holiness or Purity in CHRIST's Human Nature, than in the Nature of any of His People who are *said to be*

---

Nature," with all its inherently *sinful Propensities*," instead of saying, as he does, that " He took Man's Nature with all its *essential Properties* and *common Infirmities*, " YET WITHOUT SIN ?" *Sinfulness,* he assures us, in pa. 146, is a question " not of the *Substance,* but of the *Accidents* of Incarnation ; for " Incarnation might have been in *Adam's unfallen* Substance, as well as *Mary's fallen* Substance." Hence it appears, even from his own words, that in taking our Nature with all its " essential Properties," CHRIST was not necessarily obliged to take such Nature in a sinful or fallen state.    And as to our " Common Infirmities," " without Sin," it is manifest that *Mr. Irving* here cloaks his *real* Sentiments under the very expressions used by his Opponents, (who hold that CHRIST took a Sinless Humanity, with all its Sinless Infirmities,) because *he* secretly holds that it was " Fallen Human Nature with *all* its *Sinful Propensities,*" which CHRIST assumed, or as he elsewhere calls it, " this Nature of ours, which is *full* of Sin, and *Death,* and *Rebellion,* and *Dishonour* unto God."—(*Pref.* vii.)    Is it honest, therefore, in *Mr. Irving,* to use the terms he here does, as descriptive of that inherent *Sinfulness* of CHRIST's Human Nature, which he still secretly maintains ? In his " Orthodox Doctrine" he publicly declares, "he will not yield a jot of it, and that he will suffer the loss of all things sooner, and death itself, than suffer this Doctrine to be shaken so long as he can help it."— (111.) Whereas, in his " Solemn Declaration" he never so much as *once mentions* the *Sinfulness* of the Nature which CHRIST assumed ; or there even attempts to *describe* it by any one of the numerous *unholy* epithets whereby he but everywhere designates it in his " Orthodox Doctrine !"    In the *latter* he makes the *Sinfulness,* the *inherent Sinfulness* of the Humanity of JESUS, to be the very *Basis* of *every Doctrine* that he holds—(27, 28.) While in the *former* he never so much as *once notices it* as a Doctrine that he *now* really believes, and least of all as the very *Basis* of all others ; or " *that* which he will maintain even unto the death." Well, then, may some persons enquire, Does *Mr. Irving* now *really* hold the Inherent Sinfulness of CHRIST's Human Nature as maintained in his " Orthodox and Catholic Doctrine ?" If he *does,* why has he not, in his

regenerated of the HOLY GHOST; while it not only serves to confirm those who *know* that *in Regeneration their dead* Souls were *quickened;* that GOD *has* given them " a *new* Heart and a *new* Spirit;" that they are made " *new Creatures;*" that " *old* things have *passed away,* and behold all things are become *new;*" but it affords them additional evidence that *Mr. Irving* himself cannot be the *subject* of that scriptural Regeneration which he *denies;* neither can he spiritually *know* Him who is " the altogether lovely," (according to the literal description and the personal revelation of Him to the regenerated soul, by the SPIRIT of TRUTH,) since His Human

---

" Solemn Declaration," *openly* and *unequivocally* AVOWED it? And, if he does *not,* why has he not as *openly* and as *unequivocally* RENOUNCED it ?"

Of those other Gentlemen, too, who have " solemnly declared" that the Doctrines stated in the " Declaration" before quoted, are those which are " constantly taught" in the Church of which *Mr. Irving* is the Minister, and they are the " Missionary, Elders, and Deacons;" it may be enquired, whether *Mr. Irving* really *does* or does *not* NOW *preach,* that the Human Nature of our LORD JESUS CHRIST was, in itself, " Sinful,"—" inherently Sinful,"—having " the very same Dispositions, Propensities, and Inclinations *to evil,*" as *their* Nature has; and " Differing nothing from theirs in its alienation and guiltiness before God ?" If he *does,* how can they vindicate their " Solemn Declaration" from the charge of cloaking *Mr. Irving's* real Sentiments of the Inherent and total Sinfulness and Corruptibility of the whole Human Nature of the LORD JESUS, as elsewhere expressed ? Since all that *they* say concerning His Humanity is, that " He took *Man's Nature* with all the essential Properties and common Infirmities thereof, *yet* WITHOUT SIN !" While *Mr. Irving* expressly affirms, that " the Manhood which the SON of GOD assumed" was " FULL OF SIN," yea, " *Corrupt* to the very *Heart's Core,* and from the *centre* of its *inmost Will,* sending out *Streams* black as Hell !!!" (*Ortho. Doc.* 126.) And if he does *not,* how can *Mr. Irving* NOW *preach* either " the only *Foundation* of the Orthodox Faith," or any thing of " the Alpha and Omega, the Beginning and the Ending of the Orthodox Theology," which he makes the *inherent Sinfulness* of the Humanity of Jesus to be, in his " Orthodox and Catholic Doctrine of our Lord's Human Nature ?"

The above Gentlemen may continue to *assert,* as in their " Solemn Declaration" they have asserted, that they " *utterly detest* and *abhor* any Doctrine that would charge with Sin, original or actual, our blessed LORD and SAVIOUR JESUS CHRIST," and fancy they can exempt Him from the charge of Sin, because *Mr. Irving's* Sophistry may have led them to conclude that the *Person* of CHRIST consisted of His *Divine* Nature *only,* and that therefore " he can

Nature *Mr. Irving* affirms was "*full* of *Sin*"—"*corrupt* even to the very *Heart's Core,* and from the *centre* of its *inmost Will* sending forth Streams *black* as *Hell!!!*" (p. 126.)

"Revealed Truths," observed the very learned and reverend Preceptor of the great *Mr. Locke,** "are strange things to the natural man, and will never find acceptance with him, till his mind be suited to them by a supernatural irradiation. Heavenly things cannot be seen but by a heavenly Light. There are more *Nicodemuses* than one, who cannot unriddle the Mystery of Regeneration: they will understand nothing by it but what they can bring themselves

---

assert the Sinfulness of the whole Human *Nature* which He took, without in the least implicating Him with Sin;" yet, if they really, and in all godly simplicity and sincerity do believe, as they have avowed, that the Lord Jesus was " very God and very Man, yet ONE CHRIST," and at the same time hold with *Mr. Irving,* that His Manhood was in itself, and of itself, *inherently Sinful,* or " full of Sin," &c. as described above, they must either detest and abhor their *own* Doctrine, or deny that the *Human* Nature was *any part* of the PERSON of *their Christ !* The former would destroy their " Solemn Declaration"—while the latter would annihilate their *Soul's Salvation!*

What then becomes of this " Solemn Declaration" of " The Minister, Missionary, Elders, and Deacons of the National *Scotch* Church, Regent Square, *London;*" which professes to set forth " to all *honest* Men," an *honest* statement of the *Faith* of their *Church,* and of the preaching of their *Minister ?* Since it plainly *avows,* that the Human Nature which the SON of GOD assumed was " *without Sin*," (when *Mr. Irving* most unequivocally asserts that it was " FULL OF SIN"—*Pref.* vii.) and entirely *avoids* any honest mention whatever, of that one pre-eminently important Doctrine in *Mr. Irving's* Creed, which he assures us elsewhere is the " very Foundation Stone of the Orthodox Faith," and " of the Substance and Essence of the Orthodox Faith to hold," namely, the inherent Sinfulness of the whole Human Nature which the SON of GOD took, from the Conception in the Virgin until the Resurrection from the Tomb ! Must we not say, that such "Solemn Declaration" will stand a record on high, either of the " Strong Delusion" under which they labour who have made it ; or that, so far from its being a plain, honest, unequivocal statement of what *Mr. Irving* preaches, and the *National* SCOTCH *Church* in Regent Square believes, that it is a most delusive covering to a most Pestilent Heresy, which is secretly *held,* but is neither openly, honestly, or unequivocally *avowed ?*

And here again I would say, " Let them bring forth their witnesses that they may be justified, or let them hear and say,—It is Truth !"

---

* The Rev. *T. Cole;* the distinguished Principal of *St. Mary's Hall,* OXFORD, 1686.

unto by an outward Baptism. There is no reasoning with these men : while they live in one nature, and talk of another, they say they know not what ! It is impossible to have a real feeling of that nature which is not in us." And so it is written in that Holy Book before which *Mr. Irving* says he is " accustomed to tremble"—(and well he may, after his perilous alterations of it, and the fearful things he has spoken against the Inherent Holiness of that JESUS who is the very Spirit or Substance of it,) " the natural Man *receiveth not* the things of the SPIRIT of GOD : for they are *foolishness* unto *him;* neither *can* he *know* them, because they are spiritually discerned." 1 *Cor.* i. 14. And however *we* may be informed by *Mr. Irving* of those " high points of Truth and Reason," which he says "he is continually straining his Faculties to express ;" (145.) and of that Sphere of Thought and *Reasoning,* "into which, for our soul's good," he says " he must drag *us* up ;" (131.) it is evident enough, that a person may yet inhabit those very Regions, and in them strain his finest Faculties to express those very " high points of Truth and Reasoning" of which *Mr. Irving* speaks, and yet remain amongst those, who, in poetic language, still " blindly creep, or sightless soar ;" or, in the infallible expression of the Word of GOD, who " wander out of the Way of Understanding, and remain in the Congregation of the Dead." *Prov.* xxi. 16.

It is the bane of the professing Church of the present day, that so many attempts are made to fritter away the spirit, if not the very letter also, of such important passages of Holy Scripture as those just quoted from 1 *Cor.* ii. 14, and *John* iii. by men whose Faith standeth " in the Wisdom of Men, and not in the Power of GOD." And hence it is that a *Christianity* which is *Intellectual* but *not Spiritual;* which is acquired by natural Men as they attain any human Science; which is propagated by mere systematic Preachers, " not having the SPIRIT;" and which is received by Hearers, who have indeed a " Form of Godliness but who deny the Power," is spreading itself more rapidly, in this day of *unscriptural*

*Charity*, than many persons are aware of. " We will eat our own Bread, and wear our own Apparel, only let us be *called* by Thy Name, to take away our reproach," being very descriptive of such Persons in our day, who " say they are rich and increased with goods, and have need of nothing ; and know not that they are wretched, and miserable, and poor, and blind, and naked." " They are *of* the World," said " that disciple whom JESUS loved ;" " therefore *speak* they of the World, and the World heareth them." 1 *John* iv. 5. " We are of GOD : he that knoweth GOD, heareth us ; he that is not of GOD, heareth *not* us." " The blind may still lead the blind, until both shall fall into the ditch." " Nevertheless, the foundation of GOD standeth sure, having this seal ; the LORD knoweth them that are His."

Here let it be remembered, that the following pages were not written with any unfriendly feeling towards the Person of *Mr. Irving*, or towards the Persons of any of those Individuals who espouse his Sentiments. Doctrines, not Persons, have provoked the present Controversy ; which, it is hoped, the true Believer in the LORD JESUS CHRIST will find a plain and *earnest*, though not an angry endeavour to expose a most ruinous Error, and to defend precious Truth. The Author has studiously sought to understand the Productions he has answered ; and he has plainly and faithfully dealt with the Errors he has found ; and that, too, (as much as possible, to use *Mr. Irving's* own words,) " with forbearance to the Men, but with unsparing Destructiveness to their erroneous Doctrines." In doing which he has endeavoured, " Nothing to extenuate, nor aught set down in malice." And, so far from entertaining any uncharitable feeling towards *Mr. Irving*, he would greatly rejoice to hear (if it were the Will of GOD) that *he* really possessed *that* " Repentance which needeth not to be repented of," for all that he has *thought*, for all that he has *spoken*, and for all that he has *written*, against the *inherent Sinlessness* of GOD's *Holy Child* JESUS." Then would *such* Repentance evince itself, not in the language *Mr. Irving* uses where he speaks of Consequences if his Doctrine were false, (" If this Principle must go to the Wall, I shall go to the Wall along with it,") but in some such heart-felt, soul-felt, moving strains as these : " Oh that my Head were Waters, and mine Eyes a Fountain of Tears, that I might weep day and night" for the Blasphemies uttered in that Book, against the *inherent* Purity, and the incorruptible Humanity, of the HOLY ONE of GOD!" It being ever by the sorrowful path of " Weeping and Mourning, and Lamentation, that " the Father of Mercies" is pleased to lead to Himself those of His Children, who, like *Peter*, may have even " denied the LORD who bought them." For, " he that covereth his Sins shall not prosper : but whoso confesseth and forsaketh them shall have Mercy." *Prov.* xxviii. 13.

Of the numerous Errors opposed in the subsequent pages, but more especially that pre-eminently awful one of the Inherent Sinfulness of the Humanity of JESUS, the Author knows not in what terms sufficiently to express the utter loathing of his Soul, than by declaring, that he doth from his very Heart and Soul abhor and detest, as blasphemous and heretical, that damnable Doctrine and Position, that " every variety of *Human Wickedness*, which hath ever been realized, was inherent in the Humanity" of the SON of GOD ! ! ! Let that day be Darkness, in which so monstrous a Delusion was conceived ; and let that Night be solitary, let no joyful Voice come therein, in which so blasphemous a Notion was brought forth !

> " Union abhorr'd ! Dissimulation vain !
> Could HOLINESS embrace the *Harlot* SIN !
> Could *Life* wed *Death ?* Could GOD with *Satan* dwell ?"

O my Soul ! come not *thou* into their Secret ! Unto their Assembly my *Friends* be not ye united. For Destruction and Misery are in this way, and the way of Peace it is not. All the ways of Error are subtle ways, and they deceive but to destroy. She hath cast down many wounded ; yea, many strong men have been slain by her. Her house inclineth unto Death, and her paths unto the dead. None that go unto her return, (without Injury,) and none that die in her embrace take hold of the path of Life. Her house is the way to Hell, going down to the chambers of Death. And, as "he that wandereth out of the way of Understanding shall remain in the Congregation of the dead," Take heed *what* ye hear; and Cease thou to hear the Instruction that causeth to err from the Words of Knowledge; yea, flee from it as thou wouldest from the face of a serpent. "Avoid it, pass not by it, turn from it, and pass away."

I make no doubt in saying, (and that too in the very words which *Mr. Irving* has used of his opponents' Sentiments) "that *his* Doctrine is damnable; that to believe it is to believe a Lie; to die in the Faith of it is to die in the Faith of a Lie; and which, like every Lie, I believe will work the glory of the *Devil*, who was a Liar from the beginning, and not the glory of Jesus Christ, who is The Truth."

> "It weaves the *winding-sheet* of Souls, and lies
> Them in the Urn of *everlasting Death !*"

May the Spirit of all Truth, as the Spirit of Wisdom and of Revelation in the knowledge of the Lord Jesus Christ —and without whose Revelation no man can say that Jesus is the Lord—dispose the serious Reader of the following pages to prove all things therein, by bringing them all "to the Law and to the Testimony," and to hold fast only those things which are good; to make the Word of God his constant Study, and the Spirit of God his only Commentator; to buy the Truth and sell it not; and to "cease from Man whose breath is in his nostrils, for wherein is *he* to be accounted of !"

Reader! "Consider what I say; and the Lord give thee understanding in all things."

*December*, 1830.              W. H. C.

# OBSERVATIONS,

### &c.

---

HONOURABLE AND HONOURED FRIEND,

I MAY truly say, and in the very language of the great Apostle to the Gentiles, that I have had "great heaviness and continued sorrow in my heart" since I had the grief to hear from your own lips, that you entertained in any degree the very unscriptural, and, in my esteem, the no less dreadful and heretical Doctrine advanced by *Mr. Irving,* "the *Sinfulness* of the *Human Nature* of our LORD JESUS CHRIST;" because, if this Doctrine were true, it would not only leave *me* without any real ground of Hope, as a Sinner, but would deprive even *my honoured Friend* also of every thing but the name !

Bear with me then, my honourable Friend, while with the greatest plainness of speech I depart not from that faithfulness I owe to GOD, and that christian respect which is due to you, I comply with your request in giving you my thoughts in writing upon *Mr. Irving's* Sentiment; and more especially upon his own illustration of it, inserted in the *Third* Number of *The Morning Watch,* under the Title of "The True Humanity of CHRIST." And this unworthy offering at my hands you had received before, had I not been unexpectedly called from home, and occasionally indisposed since my return.

That the Sentiment *Mr. Irving* has advanced is of the most vital importance in his esteem, is evident, from his declaring it to be " the *Foundation* of the Orthodox Faith"—(page 421) " the *only one* Faith of the Church"—(422) "this *great Head*

B

of Orthodox Doctrine"—(422). And that every one who will not confess that " Jesus Christ is come in *sinful* Flesh, is a deceiver and Anti-Christ"—and that " God hath sent *that* Man a strong delusion that he should believe a Lie !" (424, 5.)

Where then, my honourable Friend, let me ask, where are *now* the Spirits of all those great, and wise, and holy Men of God, who, as the Ministers of Christ more especially, have adorned the Church of *England* from the first dawning of the Reformation down to the present day ; and were such strenuous Advocates for the *inherent* Holiness of the Human Nature of the Lord Jesus Christ; and who lived and died in the confirmed belief of it ? Where, for instance, is the Spirit of *that* " holy Man of God"—that highly honoured Servant of the Lord—that " burning and shining Light," in his day, the venerable *Romaine?* For *he* has expressly declared, again, and again, and again, that the Human Nature of Christ was *inherently* holy ! (See his Sermon on 2 *Cor.* v. 21.) And so momentous a Doctrine was the inherent Holiness of the Human Nature of the Lord Jesus Christ, in *Mr. Romaine's* esteem, that he shews how the whole of His *Righteousness* was founded upon it, and the *Hope* of all true Believers inseparably connected with it ! Can we then, for a single moment, suppose that God had *indeed* given up *Mr. Romaine* to such an awful state as *Mr. Irving* describes ? namely, that God should have " *sent* that Man a strong *delusion ?*" and that such a man should really have " believed a *Lie!*" (as *Mr. Irving's* statement would imply *Mr. Romaine's* Faith must have been) and that *Mr. Romaine,* after having so long preached, " through the Grace that was given to him of God," what the " Spirit of Truth" so pre-eminently blessed; and, after having lived, through the same Grace, so holy a life, and died so happy a death, that *he* should at last partake of that inconceivably awful Condemnation of *all* those who *are* so "given up ?" as we read in that appalling Scripture, 2 *Thess.* ii. 12 !

And what becomes of my honourable Friend's *own Church* also, if *Mr. Irving's* Sentiment be true ? For the Church of *England* has expressly declared, in her Fifteenth Article, that Christ was " clearly void of Sin both in His Flesh, and in His Spirit;" whereas, *Mr. Irving* asserts, that " every variety of human wickedness was *inherent* in His *Humanity!*" *Mr. Irving's* Sentiment, therefore, leaves the Church of *England* as an *Anti-Christian Church,* and *Mr. Romaine,* an *Anti-Christian Minister!* And from these conclusions there is no escape; since *Mr. Romaine* died in the firm belief of what *Mr. Irving* hesitates not to denounce as " a Lie;" and the Church of *England* still exists to maintain it in her Article.\*

But, my honourable Friend, I have greater Witness against *Mr. Irving* than that of *Mr. Romaine,* (much as I may venerate his memory)—I have higher Testimony than that of the *Church* of *England,* (much as I may prize those principal Doctrines on which she is founded, and highly as I may esteem in love, for the LORD's sake, some of the most excellent of the earth within her pale)—for, I have the Testimony of the SPIRIT OF ALL TRUTH, concerning the inherent Holiness of

---

\* The following are *some* of *Mr. Romaine's* expressions in the Sermon alluded to :

" He (CHRIST) was *conceived and born without the least taint of Corruption.*"

" He was *born holy,* and such was the *Life* of the HOLY CHILD JESUS as His *Birth* had been."

" No creature could be offered in Sacrifice to the LORD (under the ceremonial Law) if it had the least blemish or deformity. By this Type was prefigured the *perfect* SINLESS *Purity,* which was to be in the *great Sacrifice* for Sin. He was to be a *Lamb without blemish,* without the *least Spot* or *Stain* of *Sin,* either in *His* NATURE or in His *Life ;*—and such an one was the Lamb of GOD. The Apostle says expressly, 1 *Pet.* ii. 22. " He did NO Sin." And St. *John,* 1 Epis. iii. 5. speaks to Believers, " Ye know that He was manifested to take away our " Sins, and in Him is NO Sin."

"This was a known and established Truth, that in CHRIST there was NO Sin."

" He had NO *Sin* INHERENTLY in Him, but had Sin *imputed to* Him."

" In His *own Person* there was NO INHERENT SPOT or *Stain* of *Sin,* or *any such thing.*"

" Our Sins were *not* INHERENT IN CHRIST, but *imputed* TO and *laid* UPON Him."

" THE MANHOOD OF CHRIST HAD NO SIN IN IT."

" He was a *Spotless Lamb,* and therefore capable of being made Sin for us, that we might be made the Righteousness of GOD in Him."

" If you ask how the Righteousness of another can be made yours ? It must be in the same way that CHRIST was made Sin. *He* had *no Sin of His own,* and yet He was *made Sin* by *Imputation ;* and Believers have *no Righteousness* of their own, and yet are *made Righteous* by *Imputation.* CHRIST had no INHERENT SIN of His own, nor have they any *inherent Righteousness !*"

" *He* is *Sin for* them, NOT INHERENTLY, but by Imputation."

" All the Sins of the Children of *Israel* were *passed over to* the Goat; (*Lev.* xvi. 21.) but were they *put into* the Goat, or were they *inherent* in him ? No : this is too absurd to be supposed : but they were *put upon* the Goat."

" And how were they (our Sins) transferred to Him ? (CHRIST) they were *imputed,* NOT INHERENT ; they were *laid upon* Him, not INTO Him."

MR. ROMAINE on 2 *Cor.* v. 12.

the Human Nature of our LORD JESUS CHRIST, in direct opposition to the very letter and to the spirit of the contrary assertions from *Mr. Irving*. And these opposing Testimonies I shall arrange as follows :

| The SPIRIT of TRUTH declares, | *Mr. Irving* asserts, |
|---|---|
| 1. That, that which was *conceived* IN the Virgin was " OF the HOLY GHOST."      *Matt.* i. 18, 20. | 1. That " the Flesh of CHRIST was *not* in its *conception* or *generation* in a different condition from Man's Flesh"—" but was *fallen, sinful* Flesh—and *sinful* to the last." (433, 441.) |
| 2. That the *Human Body* of our LORD JESUS CHRIST was " a Body prepared *of* GOD."      *Heb.* x. 5. | 2. " That it was *Woman's Flesh,* and that is sinful—the *Seed* of *David,* and that is sinful—the *Seed* of *Abraham,* and that is sinful"—and hence, that it necessarily was " *sinful* Flesh and Blood."—(424, 431.) |
| 3. That which *was* born of the Virgin was "*That* HOLY THING."*      *Luke* i. 35. | 3. That it was " *sinful Substance,"—sinful Flesh,* as ours is, " with the *same dispositions,* and *propensities,* and *wants,* and *afflictions*—and always *sinful.*" — (424, 425.) |

---

* " But I will not suffer any Casuist or Sophist, (*Mr. Irving* says) reasoning from this, by cunning and self-deluding Art, to bring out a *Conclusion* against the *Fact*, as he calls it, of His (CHRIST'S) mortality and corruption: even though I could not refute his reasoning, which I think it not worth while to attempt, I would say, that he was both heretical and schismatical in gainsaying one of the strongest, dearest, and best defended positions of the Catholic Faith."      " *Orthodox and Catholic Doctrine*," p. 34.

Equally insufferable then, to others, must appear the " Reasonings" of *Mr. Irving*, from the text above quoted ; in which he attempts, " by cunning and self-deluding art, to bring out a CONCLUSION *against* the FACT" of the *inherent Holiness* of our LORD's Human Nature, contained in the above plain and precious declaration of the Scriptures of Truth. " Even though we could not refute his Reasoning," (which on this, as on many other occasions, refutes itself,) we must say, after reading his assertions on the opposite column, that *he* is " both heretical and schismatical in gainsaying one of the strongest, dearest, and best defended positions of the *Christian* Faith"—the *inherent Sinlessness* of " *That* HOLY THING," which was conceived, or begotten, *in* the Virgin, *of* the HOLY GHOST, and which " *also*" (though " *made* of a Woman," and " the *Seed* of the Woman") was to be called, and was called, " THE SON OF GOD."

THEORY *against* FACT, is what *Mr. Irving* would be thought to have opposed, in the above Scripture ; when, in truth, *Theory* AGAINST *Fact* is what he has *espoused ;* not only therein, but throughout his " Tractate," so falsely entitled " The *Orthodox* and *Catholic* Doctrine of our LORD's Human Nature." The oft repeated " How can *this* be,"—or " How can *that* be," " *if* CHRIST

| The SPIRIT of TRUTH declares, | Mr. Irving asserts, |
|---|---|
| 4. "In HIM is NO SIN."<br>1 *John* iii. 5. | 4. In His Humanity "*was inherent every variety of Human Wickedness*"*—that it was the *Strong-hold* of Sin, and *under its Dominion*. (422.) |
| 5. He was "HOLY, HARMLESS, UNDEFILED, SEPARATE FROM SINNERS."<br>*Heb.* vii. 26. | 5. That His "Manhood was *fallen, sinful,* and *corrupt*"—and that He *held communion* with *every impious, ungodly,* and *blasphemous chamber* of the *fallen Intellect and feeling of Men.*"† (434, 435.) |
| 6. He was "WITHOUT SIN."<br>*Heb.* iv. 15. | 6. That "His Flesh was *full of Sin*"—that "He had that *Mass of Iniquity* with which *Mr. Irving* and every sinful Man is oppressed." (423, 421). |
| 7. That HE "KNEW no Sin."<br>That HE "DID no Sin."<br>2 *Cor.* v. 21—1 *Peter* ii. 22. | 7. That "the *Flesh* of CHRIST did carry up to His *Mind every form of Seduction;*" and that, "through the faculties of the *Human Soul*, He condescended to hold *Communion* with *every impious, ungodly,* and *blasphemous chamber* of the *fallen Intellect* and *feeling of Men.*"† (426, 427.) |

\* Mr. I.'s Sermons, I. pa. 164.    † Pa. (140) II.

---

took not our *fallen* nature with all its *natural* and *inherent propensities.*"—" I WANT" *this*, and " I WANT *that*, in order " to adjust the observations to my *Feelings*, and the scale of *my Understanding*," (such for instance as " a GODHEAD not absolute," but " limited,"—a CHRIST " set up," " all intelligible," " all within the bounds of *pure Reason*"—as *Mr. Irving* sets forth in pp. 143, 144—" the *exact bearing* of the miraculous Conception," &c. which he informs us he has shewn; and those " high points of *Truth* and *Reason*, which, he says, " he is continually straining his faculties to express." (pp. 87, 145.) All these things exhibit to us the very " *Casuist* or *Sophist*" *Mr. Irving* reprehends; who, " by cunning and self-deluding art, brings out the Conclusion" of his own natural Reason against the Spirit's Revelation of the Truth of God, and the Great Mystery of Godliness, " GOD manifest in the Flesh." For the things of divine *Revelation* are only received to profit by divine *Application :* " the things of the SPIRIT of GOD" being understood only " through the Faith of the operation of GOD," on the ground of the Veracity of GOD ; and not at all through their being " adjusted to the Feelings, and to the scale of the Understanding" of the natural man ; or brought " within the bounds of pure *Reason*," as *Mr. Irving* requires, and strives in vain to obtain. The system he sets up may, I think, be not improperly designated " *Human Theory* against *Divine Fact :*" whilst " the Revelation of JESUS CHRIST" in the experience of the true Church in all ages, may be denominated, " DIVINE FACT and DIVINE ACT *against* ALL THE THEORIES IN THE WORLD."                    1 *Cor.* i. 19—24.

| The SPIRIT of TRUTH declares, | Mr. Irving asserts, |
|---|---|
| 8. That "the *Prince of this World* came, and had NOTHING in HIM." *John xiv.* 30. | 8. That " if there had not been in CHRIST's nature, *Appetites*, and *Ambitions*, and *spiritual Darkenings*, how could the *Devil* have addressed these Temptations to His *Will?*"—That His *Will* was " in *bondage* to the *Devil*, the *World*, and the *Flesh*"—the Nature *He* took, that of " the *Apostate Sinful Creature*" — Sin's " own *Strong-hold*" — under " its *dominion*"—and, unchanged " *anterior* to the *Resurrection*."* (425, 434, 435, 422.) |

---

\* Not contented with thus blaspheming that "HOLY ONE," by whose name the Children of GOD are called, *Mr. Irving* has proceeded to give us a still more awful description of *his* views of the exceeding sinfulness of the Human Nature of our LORD JESUS CHRIST, in an enlarged Edition of the Essay opposed by the above Letter, which has lately been published under the very specious and equally false Title of " *The Orthodox and Catholic Doctrine of our* LORD's *Human Nature ;*" in which, amongst other statements, are the following :

" I believe, that my LORD did bring His Divine Person into Death-possessed Humanity, into the one substance of manhood created in *Adam*, and by the fall brought into a state of resistance to, and alienation from God ; of condemnation, and proclivity to evil ; of subjection to the Devil; (2.) having met all sin, and all weakness, and all mortality, and all corruption, and all Devils, and all creature-oppression, and all creature-rebellion, *in* HIS FLESH : (8.) every variety of Human *Passion*, every variety of Human *Affection*, every variety of Human *Error*, every variety of Human *Wickedness*, which hath ever been realized, *inherent* in the Humanity, and combined against the Holiness of Him who was not only a Man, but the Son of Man, the Heir of all the Infirmities which Man entaileth upon his Children." (17.) In such a reasonable Soul, (that is, as all other men's) " liable to Temptations through the Flesh, and in such a Flesh LOVING *the* TEMPTATION *and ever conversing with the* TEMPTER, (*Mr. Irving* dares to assert the *Athanasian* Creed declares) that CHRIST subsisted." (37.) " His flesh is linked unto all material things Devil-possessed." (40.) " The same on which Satan hath triumphed ever since the fall." (40.) " The substance of his sinful Mother." (36.) "The vile substance of the Virgin." (57.) " Darkened reason, and lustful flesh." (134.) " Sin having entered into man's mind, into his flesh, into creation thereupon, They became Sin-possessed, Devil-minded, Death stricken." " And we are all of one root, of one quality, of one vileness, in the sight of GOD ; darkness and chaos, poison, and pestilence, and tempest, strife, and quarrel, and bloodshed, are amongst them." (132, 133.) " Manhood after the fall broke out into sins of every name and aggravation ; corrupt to the very heart's core, and from the *centre* of its *inmost Will* sending out *streams black* as *Hell. This* is the Human Nature which *every man* is clothed upon withal, *which the* SON OF MAN *was clothed upon withal, bristling thick and strong with Sin like the hairs upon the Porcupine*"!!! "This poisonous coat, not of Flesh merely, but of Flesh and Heart, covering and insphering, and grasping, and oppressing every person, and dragging him down

Here, my honourable Friend, we do *not* find *Mr. Irving* speaking as all well-instructed spiritual Scribes ought to speak, namely, " as of the Oracles of GOD," or " in the words which the HOLY GHOST teacheth, comparing spiritual things with spiritual,"—but we *do* find him using expressions which are at open war with both the Letter, and with the Spirit also, of those " Scriptures of Truth" which " were written for our learning," and which are " able to make us wise unto Salvation;" not through the *Reasoning* of *Man,* but " through *Faith* which is in CHRIST JESUS."  And however *Mr. Irving* may seek to reconcile his Sentiments to " the Scriptures of Truth," by the aid of his own Reasonings, such Reasonings cannot possibly be of GOD, because they are false and contradictory in themselves; and, more especially, because they oppose both the Letter and the Spirit of His Holy Word; and would make our Faith to stand in what we are assured it *ought not* to stand—" the *Wisdom* of *Men*"—and would lead us away from what we are also informed it *ought* to stand in—namely, " the *Power* of GOD."  " To the Law, and to the Testimony;

---

out of light into Hell's nethermost pit of darkness," (which, in the same page he also calls) " the teeming Fountain of the Heart's vileness"—" the *Augean Stable* of Human Wickedness"—containing " furious wild Beasts of human Passions,"—" the Dogs, and the Lions, and the Unicorns, and the many strong Bulls of *Bashan,*"—the Sins of that Substance which he took—in which he heard " the roaring violence of those Passions more fearful than the cave of *Eolus*"— and wherein CHRIST saw " those fearful shapes of darkness like *Pandemonium* disclosed" ! ! ! (126, 127.)   And in the close of the latter page he adds :

" I believe it to be MOST *Orthodox*, and of the *Substance* and *Essence* of the *Orthodox Faith*, to hold that CHRIST could say *until His Resurrection*, NOT I, BUT SIN THAT TEMPTETH ME IN MY FLESH ; just as *after* the Resurrection he could say, " I am separate from Sinners."   And, moreover, I believe that the *only difference* between His *Body* of *Humiliation* and His *Body* of *Resurrection* is in *this very thing*, that SIN INHERED *in the Human Nature, making it mortal and corruptible, till that very time that* HE *rose from the dead :* AND IF THIS PRINCIPLE MUST GO TO THE WALL, I SHALL GO TO THE WALL ALONG WITH IT"! !

And who that knows the " Grace of GOD in truth," after having read the foregoing Quotations from *Mr. Irving's* pen, but will consider that he has as justly described his *own* condition as that of any of those other persons who were in the eye of his mind, or were exclusively intended by him when he wrote the following words, with which he closes his Publication which is the immediate Subject of these Notes : " Ah ! it is a fearful siege which is at present carrying on against the very citadel of GOD's own HOLY BEING, and man's free inheritance in His Grace ; and WE, who should have been as one man to defend GOD's HOLY BEING, and our own goodly inheritance in His Grace, are like the sons of EPHRAIM *drunken*, but *not* with *strong drink,*—DRUNKEN WITH DELUSION AND THE CUP OF ERROR"! !                *Orthodox Doctrine,* 154.

if they speak not according to this Word, it is because there is no light in them."*

In declaring the Human Nature of CHRIST to be " sinful, like ours"—with the very same dispositions and propensities, both in Body and Soul"—" differing in no degree whatever from ours in its alienation and guiltiness"—(434) but having " every variety of human Wickedness which hath been realized, or is possible to be realized, inherent in His Humanity"— " His Soul, a sinful Soul"—" His Body, a Mass of Iniquity," and that " even to the last,"—*Mr. Irving* has not only opposed all those before-mentioned Scriptures that so expressly assert the *inherent Holiness* of THAT, which is as expressly declared to have been " conceived OF the HOLY GHOST"— (*Matt.* i. 18, 20.) of " that true Tabernacle which GOD pitched, and not Man"—(Heb. viii. 2. with John i. 14.) but he thereby exposes the " HOLY ONE OF GOD"—" GOD's HOLY CHILD JESUS"—to every one of those awful descriptions we have in the Word of GOD of the sinfulness and vileness of the miserable Sons and Daughters of fallen Man! For instance :— that the " *Mind* is carnal," and at " Enmity against GOD ;" " not subject to the Law of GOD, neither indeed can be ;" the *Heart*, " deceitful above all things, and desperately wicked ;" every Imagination " of it evil, only evil, and that continually ;" all evil thoughts, Adulteries, Murders, and the whole Catalogue of human Crime lodging in the Heart (their home) before they proceeded out of it—the *Will*, in bondage to the World, the Flesh, and the Devil—the *Understanding*, " darkness"—the *Affections*, " earthly, sensual, devilish"—†

---

* He is " had in reputation, both for wisdom and honour" in the Church of GOD, who has observed, in the close of the Preface to his Body of Divinity, " When men leave the sure Word, the only Rule of Faith and Practice, and follow their own Fancies, and the dictates of their carnal minds, they must needs go wrong, and fall into labyrinths, out of which they cannot find their way : to the Law and to the Testimony, if they speak not according to this Word, it is because there is no Light in them."

" Let us, therefore, ' Search the Scriptures,' to see whether the Doctrines advanced are according to them or not."          Dr. GILL.

† Awful as this representation may appear, *Mr. Irving* has greatly exceeded it in the various descriptions of the innate (and may I not add, of the *Satanic*) " vileness" he has given us of the Human Nature which the SON OF GOD assumed; calling it, as he does, not only a " Mass of Iniquity,"—" Sin possessed,"—" Manhood corrupt to the very heart's core, and from the centre of its inmost Will sending forth streams black as Hell," &c.—but that it was

In a word—that GOD's "HOLY CHILD JESUS," being just as sinful, as to His Human Nature, must have been just as *hateful* to GOD as any other sinful creature—and "a Child of Wrath even as others"—for, between Him and them, *Mr. Irving* declares there was not the smallest possible difference "in alienation and guiltiness"—"*every variety* of human Wickedness which *hath been realized,* or is possible *to be* realized, being *inherent* in *His Humanity!*" Words, these, which set forth the most complete Picture of a Child of the Devil that I ever met with from the pen, or ever heard from the tongue, of any uninspired Man! and which attribute all this Wickedness to "*That* HOLY THING" of which the HOLY GHOST, the *very* SPIRIT of all HOLINESS, is declared to have been the Author or Begetter!"*

---

under the *Dominion* or the "*Oppression* of the *Devil,*"—"*Devil-minded,*"—and "*Devil-possessed,*"—"*loving* the *Temptation,* and *ever conversing with the*TEMPTER,"—until, at length, (in the moment of the Resurrection, and not before,) the *Divine* Nature of CHRIST, " with the weak instruments of *fallen Humanity* did *combat* and CAST THE DEVIL OUT!!" (67.) And yet, such is *Mr. Irving's* manifest contradiction of himself in the very same breath, that his very next words to the above, are these: " His Humanity, though in itself and of itself *like ours* in *all respects,* was *therefore* not chargeable *with any Sin,* with any *moral Corruption,* was *holy, blameless, without spot;* and IT IS A MOST CAPITAL ERROR TO BELIEVE OTHERWISE. *Otherwise* I have *never believed, otherwise* I have *never thought* of believing, *otherwise* I have *never spoken, otherwise* I have *never* been *tempted to speak."* (67.)

Some Persons, however, have dared to believe, that *Mr. Irving has been* TEMPTED to *assert* those very things he here denies! 2 *Cor.* xi. 14, 15.

* To obviate this objection as much as possible, and at the same time to save the *appearance* of the Miracle in the Conception and Birth of our LORD, *Mr. Irving* has recourse to some expedients that utterly fail him when brought to the test.

Passing by the first, which relates to the *Divine* Nature of our LORD " becoming intelligible," or " within the bounds of pure Reason," (as *Mr. Irving* calls what he thinks he has accomplished through his " unsober Fancy" having " constructed a *God* for himself," in order to answer such purpose, and which he makes out to be a sort of *inferior God,* and denominates " a Subsistence" existing " before all worlds,"—" Christhood,"—" *The* Christ,"—" *Godhead* subsisting under an intelligible Form," &c. &c. pp. 143, 144, 145, a monstrous notion of his which I intend exposing at large in some other Note, or Postscript to this Letter) I can only notice *here* that other expedient, which relates to *That* HOLY THING which was conceived *in* the Virgin, *of* the HOLY GHOST, made of a *Woman,* and which *also* was called " THE SON OF GOD."

In page 87 of his " Orthodox and Catholic Doctrine of our LORD's Human Nature," *Mr. Irving* informs us of his having elsewhere shewn " the exact bearing of the miraculous Conception." In page 34, he acquaints us with this grand Secret, namely, that " the Power causing Conception was of the HOLY

But can my honourable Friend for one moment entertain the Idea, the truly horrible Idea, that the *Mind* of our LORD JESUS CHRIST was " Enmity against GOD !" His *Heart* "deceitful above all things, and desperately wicked !" " Every *Imagination* of it evil, only evil, and that continually !" HIS *Understanding* darkness ! HIS *Will* in bondage, and under " the oppression of the World, the Flesh, and the Devil !" HIS *Affections* " earthly, sensual, devilish !" HIMSELF hateful *to* and *hating* GOD—and "a Child of Wrath, even as others ! !" And yet, *all* this, and *much more* than this, *Mr. Irving* maintains, when he declares that " *every variety* of

---

GHOST,"—and " *all that followed* upon the Conception was of the Virgin *Mary*,"—" and is ascribed to *her* as *to any other Woman in the case of any other Child*." In this way *Mr. Irving* would lay the axe of his unhallowed Reason to the very root of *divine Truth* in the *divine Mystery* of the Incarnation of THE SON OF GOD; or turn in that " wild Boar of the forest," as I may say, which would root out the Mystery altogether.

On the ground of the before-mentioned assertion, that Power only was given to the Virgin to conceive, I would ask, What very great difference was there between the Conception of the *Virgin* and that of *Sarah*, or that of *Elizabeth?* Neither *Sarah*, nor *Elizabeth*, could have conceived after the ordinary course of nature, because of their great age and sterility ; and *Mary* could not by reason of her virginity. It was evidently an effect above all human power, that *Sarah* should conceive when she was " barren" and " past age," being " *ninety* years old." Equally so was it that *Elizabeth* should conceive when she also was " barren," and " well stricken in years;" and both *Sarah* and *Elizabeth*, as well as *Abraham* and *Zacharias*," as good as dead." And in the above explanation of " the exact bearing of the miraculous Conception," it was no more than " an effect above all human energy," in the Conception of the *Virgin !* The means by which the *Virgin* became fruitful, *Mr. Irving* tells us, was, by " a power from the HOLY GHOST." And is it not expressly " noted in the Scriptures of Truth," that *Sarah* herself also *received Strength* to conceive seed, and was delivered of a Child when she was past age? (*Heb.* xi. 11.) If, then, the whole of the miracle lay, as *Mr. Irving* plainly shews he believes it did, in a mere operation of Divine Power, by which the Virgin conceived of her own " sinful substance" a sinful offspring, I must yet further inquire, What very great difference is there between *her* Conception and that of any other Mother who has ever yet existed, or ever will exist? The Power causing Conception, even in every ordinary case, is evidently of the LORD : for " the Fruit of the Womb is His reward :" and He it is " who maketh even the barren woman to keep house—a joyful mother of children." *Ps.* cxiii. 9. *Ps.* cxxvii. 3. *Gen.* iii. 16. *Gen.* xxx. 2.

In furthering this view *Mr. Irving* but every where asserts, that " *that* which was conceived *in* the Virgin, (and which is so expressly declared in the Word of GOD to have been *of* the HOLY GHOST, and *of* whom the Virgin was " found with Child," *Matt.* i. 18.) was not in the smallest degree inherently holy, or possessed of a purity of nature which the Law of GOD approves, or like the Holy Generator of whom it was begotten ; but was just as sinful, vile, and

human Wickedness was inherent in His Humanity"—" His Soul, a sinful Soul," and " His Flesh, sinful Flesh," " always such"—and " even to the last." And as I know of no Records that set forth " Human Wickedness" in " *all* its varieties," as do the " Scriptures of Truth," I must here maintain, that all the awful descriptions of the sinfulness and vileness of the Souls and Bodies of all the Wicked Men of whom we read therein, (not excepting even Idolatry—all the Abominations in *Ezekiel's* Vision of the Chambers of Imagery—all the Enormities of the *Beast,* and of the *False Prophet*—and even the unpardonable Sin against the HOLY GHOST—these being among the Varieties of Human Wickedness) must *all* be just as applicable, on *Mr. Irving's* Hypothesis, to " GOD'S HOLY CHILD JESUS," as they could have been to those particular Individuals concerning whom they were in the first instance declared, or made known, in the Book of GOD :— CHRIST Himself is *personally* made a *Sinner,* (for the Act of either Nature is predicable of His complex Person,) and both the FATHER and the HOLY GHOST are made to be the *Authors* or *Parents* of this inherent sinfulness—(since the formation of the Human Nature of CHRIST in the Virgin is attributed to them, and not to any *human* operation whatever.)

*Mr. Irving* manifestly makes CHRIST's Human Nature to have been the very *Essence* of all sinfulness—and CHRIST

---

corrupt, as any others of the human race that are all " conceived in sin and shapen in iniquity :" and thereby he places the ALMIGHTY GENERATOR of " that HOLY THING which was born of the Virgin," far below the level of every sinful Human Parent in the world ; yea, and even lower than the very " Beasts that perish ;" since one and all of them actually beget their own issue *in their own likeness,* after *their own image;* whereas, *Mr. Irving* makes the issue of the HOLY GHOST to be the very essence of all sinfulness,—" Sin-possessed,"— " Devil-minded,"—" Devil-possessed !" And as such, much more like Satan, " Great Sin-Originator," as *Mr. Irving* calls him, than like the SPIRIT of all HOLINESS—the SPIRIT OF GOD. Thus, *Mr. Irving's* expedients, by which he thinks to *explain* " the exact bearing of the miraculous Conception," and to make " *all* things *intelligible,* or within the bounds of pure *Reason,*" are shewn to be Rocks of Presumption, to which his own " unsober Fancy" is continually leading him, to the shipwreck of his *Faith* and *Hope,* and of the *Faith* and *Hope* . of all those who believe with him.      " Without controversy, however, great is the Mystery of Godliness : GOD was manifest in the Flesh," 1 *Tim.* iii. 16.

> " Let *Jews* on their own *Law* rely,
> And *Greeks* of *Wisdom* boast ;
> I LOVE TH' INCARNATE MYSTERY,
> And *there* is fix'd *my* Trust."      WATTS.

Himself, through having a Nature so exceedingly sinful,
" through the faculties of the Human Soul, to have *held
communion*" with every Sin in every Sinner! And yet,
*Mr. Irving* asserts, that CHRIST *did* NO *Sin!* What palpable contradiction is this! It is most evident that *Mr. Irving*
makes CHRIST to BE something, in order to DO something.
He makes *Him* to BE *inherently sinful* in order that *He*
might *hold Communion* with all Sinfulness inherent in all
Sinners! And this he tells us CHRIST condescended to do;
and yet, he says, HE DID NO SIN! Now, if Communion be
(as it is) a Fellowship or Agreement, (or a *coming into one,*
as I might term it) with approbation or delight between the
parties communing, and CHRIST did really hold with Sinners
the Communion that *Mr. Irving* declares He did, He must
have really " come into their Secret" with approbation,
through the inherent sinfulness of His Human Nature; (His
human Will being " always of itself inclined to *do* evil,"
*Mr. Irving* says, 424, 426,) and as the LORD " searches the
Heart and tries the reins," and informs us that the very
*thought* of Foolishness is Sin ; that Covetousness is Idolatry ;
that Hatred is Murder, &c. for *Mr. Irving* to say that any
one so inherently sinful, and holding Communion with all sinfulness, was not *Himself* a *Sinner,* is to argue such entire
Ignorance of what Sin is in the sight of GOD's holy Law, as
I should not have expected, even " in these most Ignorant
days," (as *Mr. Irving* calls them,) from any one professing
to be an Evangelical Minister of the High Church of *Scotland:* or indeed of any truly convinced and truly converted
Sinner, who had ever " seen an end of all Perfection," knowing "GOD's Commandment to be exceeding broad :" and who
had ever really " believed in the LORD JESUS CHRIST to the
saving of his Soul."*

---

* The Saints of GOD are exhorted in His Word to have " no Fellowship
with the unfruitful works of darkness," and to " be separate" from those who
do; (*Eph.* v. 11.) whereas, if CHRIST really had " every variety of human
*Passion,* every variety of human *Affection,* every variety of human *Error,* every
variety of human *Wickedness,* which hath ever been realized, inherent in His
Humanity," (as *Mr. Irving* assures us he had ; *Ortho. Doc.* p. 17.) and that
" through the Faculties of the human Soul," He actually " *held Communion* with
every impious, ungodly, and blasphemous Chamber in the fallen intellect and
feeling of men"—it is evident that the LORD's CHRIST did what the LORD's
*Saints* are exhorted not to do : the " Throne of Iniquity *has* Fellowship with

I am aware, my honoured Friend, of some of the means *Mr. Irving* has recourse to, in order, as he thinks, to avoid the charge of his making CHRIST a Sinner ; but they are all utterly insufficient to answer such an end :—for we must never forget, that *Sin* is not that changeable, trifling, accommodating thing which *Mr. Irving*, or any other person might attempt to make it ; extending only to the mere outward acts of the Life ; but that it is " that abominable thing that GOD hates," the transgression of that holy and righteous Law under which man was created ; which extends to all the Thoughts and Intents of the Heart ; which requires that we should BE *holy*, as well as ACT *righteously*—since all *unrigh*teousness is sin, as well as all *transgression* : all coming short of the requirement " Be ye holy," in every Thought of the heart, as well as " Be ye righteous," in every Word and Work in the Life ; for " the Law is holy, and the Commandment is holy, and just, and good." And for *Mr. Irving* to say that he does not make CHRIST a Sinner, after he has declared the following things concerning Him ; namely, that

" CHRIST took our fallen nature" into union with His GODHEAD— (434, 441) our fallen nature, with all its natural and inherent propensities," —(434)—that CHRIST " came in that nature which sinned, and which for sinning was accursed to death. Death being the proper penalty of Sin, the sign of GOD's Holiness and Justice upon a sinning man, is not to be reached or come at by any person, otherwise than through the way of sin," (436)— that " His Human Nature differed nothing from ours, in its alienation and guiltiness," (434)—that it was " Humanity fallen, sinful, and under the sentence of death," (437)—that " He was in fallen Humanity, and liable to Death," (439)—that " every variety of Human Wickedness was inherent in His Humanity"—that " His Flesh was full of Sin," (423)—a " Mass of Iniquity," (421)—His Body and Soul " the Strong-hold of Sin," and both under its dominion, (422)—His Will contrary to that of the Father—rebellious—at variance with, and at enmity against Him, (434)—a Bond-will— lying under Bondage—and that Bondage " the oppression of the Devil, the World, and the Flesh,"—(435) that, " when CHRIST took Human Nature

---

GOD," and GOD with it, (*Ps.* xciv. 20.) Righteousness *hath* fellowship with Unrighteousness, " Light *has* communion with Darkness—CHRIST *has* concord with *Belial !*" For " in such a reasonable Soul, liable to Temptations through the Flesh, and in such a Flesh, *loving* the *Temptation*, and *ever conversing with the* TEMPTER, (*Mr. Irving* pretends the *Athanasian* Creed declares, although it is *his own* assertion, that) CHRIST subsisted ! ! !" *Ortho. Doc.* p. 37.

After this manner *Mr. Irving* interprets the opinions of Men : after this manner he interprets the Creed of the *Scotch Church:* and in this way he wrests the Scriptures of Truth, to his own destruction"—if GRACE prevent not!

He took it fallen, with all its Ills, with all its Griefs, with all its Darkness, with all its Wretchedness, with all its Punishments; the complete Orb of its Action and its Passion took He, All-inclusive, All-continent"—(444) that there were " in CHRIST's nature. Appetites, and Ambitions, and spiritual Darkenings"—and " at all times"—(425) that " certainly there was a Will in Him which He contradistinguisheth from the Will of the FATHER; and which, *I say*, was the Will of the Flesh; which in itself is contrary to the Will of the FATHER"—(424) that " the Will of the Flesh is to do all those things" mentioned in *Gal.* v. 19. as the fruits of the Flesh —(426) " that His Soul descended into Hell (Hades), proved it to be a fallen Soul"—and that " His Flesh was corruptible, proved it to be fallen Flesh to the last"—(441) that " His Substance was sinful Substance"— (424) His Flesh " sinful Flesh as ours is,"—(425) " Woman's Flesh, and that is sinful,"—like *Mary's, David's,* and *Abraham's*—(424) that " when Human Nature was sentenced in the person of *Adam* to death, it was all sentenced, every particle of it whatever;"—(436) that " certainly He (CHRIST) was made under the Law, (*Gal.* iv. 4.); and that the Law is not for a righteous *thing* but for a sinful *thing*"—(424) " that every passage of Scripture which declares CHRIST to have come in the Flesh, which declareth the WORD to be made Flesh, which declareth GOD to be manifested in the Flesh, is a proof total and complete, that He came in *sinful* Flesh," (423). " And in the face of all these certainties, if a man will say, that His Flesh was not sinful Flesh as ours is, with the same dispositions, and propensities, and wants, and afflictions, then *I say*, that GOD hath sent that man strong delusion, that he should believe a Lie"!! (425.)

For *Mr. Irving* to make all these assertions concerning the LORD JESUS CHRIST, (and many similar ones elsewhere, that might be mentioned) and then to say that he does not thereby make Him a Sinner, and that " only *Railers* can *utter* it, only *Fools* can *take it in,* (421) is, not only to sit in the " Scorner's Chair"—to give us another sad, sad proof of the truth of those solemn words from the lips of that " HOLY ONE" whom the FATHER " delighteth to honour," but whom *Mr. Irving's* statements would so pre-eminently degrade—(for a " degradation" even *Mr. Irving himself* acknowledges it to be, though he calls it a " self-inflicted" one, 422.)—" If, therefore, the *Light* that is in thee be *Darkness,* HOW GREAT *is* that *Darkness!*" *Matt.* vi. 23.*

---

* Did Mr. *Irving's* CHRIST ever *covet,* or not? If He did *not,* how can it be said that " *Every* variety of human wickedness was inherent in His Humanity!" since Covetousness is evidently a human wickedness! If He *did* —then, He sinned: for the Apostle *Paul* assures us that he " had not known lust except the law had said, Thou shalt not *covet.*" And " Sin," we are assured, " is the transgression of the Law;" either in a way of omission, or of commission: all *unrighteousness* being sin, as well as all transgression. 1 *John* v. 17.

There are some persons I have lately heard of—but of whom I should have hoped " better things"—who, having

---

*Mr. Irving* must therefore deny his darling theme—the Inherent Sinfulness of CHRIST's Human Nature—or be guilty of the acknowledged Blasphemy of making CHRIST a Sinner. In the former case, his *Book* becomes the sacrifice—but in the latter—*Himself!* Since in page 421 of " the *Morning Watch,*" he asserts what he repeats in page 2 of his " *Orthodox Doctrine*"—" If, indeed, we made CHRIST a *Sinner,* then all Creeds were at an end, and all Churches ; and we were worthy to die the death of Blasphemers, to be stoned by the multitude in the open face of day. But that," he says, " is out of the question : only Railers can utter it, only Fools (in the latter work it is altered to " only ignorant persons") can take it in."

It is *Mr. Irving,* however, who " can utter it," and they are *Mr. Irving's* friends who " can take in"—That " CHRIST took our fallen nature, with all its natural and inherent propensities."—88. " The very same in substance with that which we possess"—" which is full of sin, and death, and rebellion, and dishonour unto *God.*"—*Preface* vii.—

That CHRIST's " Human Nature was held of sinful *Adam :*—he being the Lump of which He took it."—151. That " there is but one Human Nature ; it is not thine, it is not mine, it is not His ; it is the common unity of our being." —95. That " we are all of one root, of one quality, of one vileness in the sight of GOD."—133. That his LORD " did bring His Divine Person into Death-possessed humanity, into the one substance of mankind created in *Adam,* and by the Fall brought into a state of resistance to and alienation from GOD, of condemnation and proclivity to evil, of subjection to the Devil."—2. " That the substance of CHRIST's Human Nature, both the fleshly visible part, and the invisible reasonable part, was of the same nature with ours, as He took it, and as He bore it about with Him all His days : defined *per se,* on its own proper qualities, it was the very same with all the rest of the Brethren, the very substance which fell in *Adam.*"—108. " That His Flesh was accursed in the loins of our first Parents"—and that " He died by the common property of flesh to die."—Mr. I.'s *Sermons,* vol. I. (140) xxxi.—

That CHRIST " must have been made by His Human Nature liable to, and inclined to, all those things which the Law interdicted"—10. That He was " generated a very man of flesh of sin"—13. " Flesh full of Sin"—That the flesh of CHRIST had " the root of sin" in it—152. That it was the " Strong-hold of sin"—4. Every variety of human wickedness inherent in the Humanity"—17. That " His flesh did carry up to His Mind (in the " Orthodox Doctrine" it is " to *Him,*") every form of seduction." That " through the faculties of the Human Soul (so inherently sinful as before stated) He held communion with every variety of human Wickedness." That " through the Fall, CHRIST's Human Nature was brought into a state of resistance to, and alienation from GOD, of condemnation and proclivity to evil, of subjection to the Devil"—2. That His body and soul were " the Strong-hold of Sin," and both under its dominion—4. That " His flesh is the same on which *Satan* hath triumphed ever since the Fall"—40. That it is " united unto all material things, Devil-possessed"— unto Creation " Sin-possessed, Devil-minded, Death-stricken"—40, 132. " Corrupt to the very heart's core, and from the centre of its inmost Will sending out streams black as Hell. This is the Human Nature which every man is clothed upon withal, which THE SON OF MAN was clothed upon withal, bristling thick and strong with Sin like the hairs upon the Porcupine ! !"—126—

recently embraced *Mr. Irving's* sentiments, hesitate not to assert, that, theretofore they had been " walking in the dark," but that " *now, Mr. Irving's* Doctrine had brought them " into Light;" yet surely, my honoured Friend, it ought to demand some attention from all those persons who have made such an assertion, (and especially from such as call themselves Members of the Established Church,) that the Doctrine they have so recently espoused, makes their *Church* to be an *Anti-christian* Church, as I have before shewn; and their

---

That " in such a reasonable soul," (as any other man's) " liable to temptation through the flesh; and in such a flesh," (as any other man's) " loving Temptation, and ever conversing with the Tempter—CHRIST subsisted"—37.

Hence it appears, from *Mr. Irving's* own statements, that, to be possessed of a nature in which was " inherent every variety of human Wickedness," which was " naturally unholy, alienated from GOD, and rebellious—inclined to every evil that the Law interdicted—which was Sin-possessed, Devil-minded, Death-stricken, and Devil-possessed—which was corrupt to the heart's core, and from its inmost Will sending out streams black as Hell—in a state of resistance to, and alienation from God, of condemnation and proclivity to evil—of subjection to the Devil—loving the Temptation, and ever conversing with the *Tempter*."—That, to be possessed of *such* a nature, is *not sinful* in the sight of God, nor such as will subject him who hath it to the *charge* of sin; or out of his own mouth *Mr. Irving* stands convicted of Blasphemy, and has adjudged himself " worthy to die the death of all Blasphemers," for having " made CHRIST a Sinner"—Whoever may be " the *Railers* that utter it," whoever will be the *Fools* that take it in !"

*Mr. Irving's* Faith and Hope, and the Faith and Hope of *Mr. Irving's* friends, may *now* stand in such an exceedingly sinful, in such an inherently wicked Object as he has pourtrayed in the Essay opposed by the above Letter, and in the second edition of that Essay, "The Orthodox and Catholic Doctrine of our LORD's Human Nature," (daubed over as it has been with the untempered mortar of a pretended, unscriptural, and most delusive Holiness) but the day will come—" and what if it be nigh, even at the doors"—when "every man's work shall be made manifest: for the day shall declare it, because it shall be revealed by fire: and the fire shall try (i. e. prove) every man's work, of what sort it is," (1 *Cor.* iii. 13.) *Then,* " when God shall lay judgment to the line, and righteousness to the plummet; and the hail shall sweep away their refuge of lies, and the waters shall overflow their hiding-place," (*Isa.* xxviii. 15, 17.) In that day will *Mr. Irving's* heart give utterance, (but with very different feelings) to those words of his on pa. 115. (and Oh that it might be by the constraints of divine Mercy !) " I am forlorn. Woe is me! for CHRIST hath sealed my doom, and hath barred the gates of Hope upon fallen, sinful man! Oh who will translate me into the realm of Hope !"—115. For, of the Faith and Hope *Mr. Irving* sets before us, in *his* CHRIST with a *sinful manhood*, even Charity herself would proclaim,

" *Such* FAITH and HOPE can end but in Despair,
'Tis there they *find* them, and—must *leave* them there !"

*Prov.* xiv. 12. xvi. 25.

most renowned *Ministers* to be *Anti-christian* also! And, as it is still *possible* to " put Darkness for Light, and Light for Darkness," those very solemn words of the LORD to the Persons who do so, ought never to be forgotten : " Behold, all ye that *kindle* a *Fire*, that compass yourselves about with Sparks ; *walk* in the *light* of *your Fire*, and in the Sparks that *ye* have kindled. *This* shall *ye* have at *Mine* hand—*ye shall lie down in Sorrow !*" And this " lying down in Sorrow," I am fully assured would be *my* hopeless condition to all eternity, if indeed *I* were to be so left of GOD as to embrace *Mr. Irving's* Sentiments, and to live and die in the belief of so monstrous a Doctrine, so awful a Delusion, as the *Sinfulness* of the *Human Nature* of our LORD JESUS CHRIST! With this confidence in my Heart, my honoured Friend need not be surprised that I should feel great sorrow of Spirit on account of any I have known in the LORD, who have become entangled in the mazes of *Mr. Irving's* Errors : for although I know, " and am persuaded of the LORD," that no Error shall be permitted of Him to deceive any of His Elect to their *final ruin,* I also know that it is by the sorrowful path of " Weeping, and Mourning, and Lamentation," that the LORD is pleased to restore those of His Family who have fallen into such Errors as *Mr. Irving* maintains : and *such* Sorrow, on such an account, I could have wished an " abiding in the Truth" might have spared them.*

---

* How much of divine truth by *divine* teaching could such persons have ever *really known*, who, after having sat for years beneath the Ministry of " faithful men of God," whose word they own was blest of GOD to the regeneration and consolation of their souls, can *now* turn aside from the Soul-saving, Soul-comforting truths such holy men of GOD proclaimed, and still proclaim, as founded upon, or manifested through, the immaculate Purity, or inherent Holiness of GOD's HOLY CHILD JESUS—can *now* so cordially embrace those Soul-distressing, Soul-destroying Errors which *Mr. Irving* holds forth as centering in the " inherently sinful," " Sin-possessed," " Devil-minded," and " Devil-possessed Humanity" of the " Apostate Creature" he declares CHRIST's Human Nature to have been, from the first moment of its conception in the Virgin, to the very last instant of its lying in the Tomb ! (yea, and even *now it is in Heaven*, if we are to be guided by *Mr. Irving's* interpretation on pp. 119, 121, that the communication of Holiness to it were making the *Amalgam* he reprobates.)

When we remember those gracious words of the LORD JESUS (" that great Shepherd of the sheep,") " My sheep *hear* my voice, and I know them, and they follow ME : but a *Stranger* will they *not* follow, but will flee from him, for they know not (i. e. they *approve* not of) the voice of Strangers," (*John* x. 5.) what can we say of such persons but what His faithful servant *Paul* did

---

of those bewitched or fascinated *Galatians* we read of in his day, *Gal.* iii. 1. " I stand in doubt of you!" Or, are those solemn words recorded by " that disciple whom JESUS loved," in 1 *John* ii. 19. more applicable to the case?

Hath the thought never crossed the minds of such individuals, that *if* their *former* Ministers were *indeed* WRONG, (so dreadfully erroneous as to be *justly* denounced by *Mr. Irving*—" Heretics"—Men " to whom even GOD Himself hath sent a strong Delusion that they might believe a Lie," because they maintain the inherent Holiness of our LORD's Human Nature, which *Mr. Irving* declares to be a " Doctrine that is damnable," p. 141) that such Ministers were so *dreadfully erroneous* at that very period when " the SPIRIT of TRUTH" so abundantly blest their Ministry to such Seceder's souls? And that if *Mr. Irving be right*, he has but *very recently* become so; the doctrine he now espouses being, as it were, " but of yesterday,"—of only three or four years publicity at most (I believe) although he says, so much of his having *ever* been a faithful Son of an *Orthodox* Church! A Church which, I apprehend, must either very soon RE-nounce *her own* Creed or DE-nounce *his*. 1 *Kings* xviii. 21.

Perhaps it is not generally known to the Individuals I am now referring, that " from his Childhood," *Mr. Irving* has " never had any misgivings concerning this, that CHRIST took our *fallen* nature!" (p. 67.) If so, *Mr. Irving* must, even at that period, have been " spiritual," or " born of God," or else *his* faith of " Childhood," like other Children's faith, was but the natural belief of the natural or unregenerate mind: and, *if* such *then, such* it is *now*, and *ever hath been!* But if we suppose *Mr. Irving* to have been *really* regenerated in his Childhood, and that he *did* then *really* believe with such an unshaken Faith as to have had no misgivings concerning the Doctrine he now preaches, how could *he* as a CHRISTIAN, have conscientiously associated for so many years with any of the Individuals he now denounces as " Heretics ;" speaking against them in no very charitable strains, when he says they are " under a strong Delusion from GOD that they should believe a Lie,"—" Malicious Men! wicked Railers !" &c. &c. and then " with stern authority," enjoining Christians " not to receive such into their houses, nor bid them GOD speed, lest they be partakers of their evil deeds." (21.) Or how could *Mr. Irving*, as a MINISTER, have been *faithful* in his office, if *from his Childhood* he so firmly believed in the Doctrine which he *now* declares to be the *Foundation* of the Orthodox Faith,"—the " *one* ONLY *Faith* of the Church,"—when it is manifest that he *maintained it not* in public until within these very few years past? How could his Ministry, even on his own shewing, have set forth " the *Foundation* of the Orthodox Faith," or even *any part* of it, (if *that* be the *whole*, as he states it is) during all those previous years in which it is evident he did *not preach* it? Or, if he *did*, how very cold must have become that zeal for the Truth of GOD which *once* animated the Church of SCOTLAND, in having so long " winked at" one of the most destructive Heresies that ever merited or received her severest censure! " *How is the Gold become dim !*"

" To know and to understand *how* the SON OF GOD took *sinful* Flesh, and yet was *sinless*, (*Mr. Irving* says) is the Alpha and Omega, the Beginning and the Ending of Orthodox Theology." pa. 18. " *I say*, (he observes, pa. 86.) He took sinful flesh, and yet was sinless ; and, moreover, *I say* that He died, and yet was sinless. If any man say that this is a matter of mere words, I tell him that he hath yet to learn the Alphabet of his Theology." What then hath *Mr.*

the hard Speeches he has made against those who say it *does*: and fully aware that he has made many unscriptural and truly contradictory statements respecting the Holiness of the LORD JESUS CHRIST: and that he has declared in the publication alluded to, that "to *know* and to *understand how* the SON OF GOD took sin-*ful* Flesh and yet was sin-*less*, is the Alpha and the Omega, the Beginning and the Ending, of Orthodox Theology," 422.—(thereby making that darling Theme of his the very *Acmé* of *all Knowledge,* which, a much greater Divine than *Mr. Irving* ever was, or perhaps ever will be—*Mr. Romaine*—has denounced as the greatest of absurdities; yea, as Blasphemy!) and not to dwell upon these remarks of *Mr. Irving's,* which shew how he wishes to reduce all matters respecting the " great Mystery of Godliness" to his own Reason,* (or what he falsely terms, " knowledge or experience," p. 421.) and to the exclusion of Faith; and how he thinks that *he* has attained to the perfect knowledge of that Mystery, when he speaks of having shewn "the exact bearing of the miraculous Conception"—I observe, that *Mr. Irving* necessarily *denies* the real knowledge of the Holiness of CHRIST, because he rejects the only way by which *we* can possess it, (i. e. by believing, as the Virgin did, that, as "all things are possible with GOD," so that which was conceived within her was of " the HOLY GHOST," —that it was " THAT HOLY THING"—and that it also should be called " the SON OF GOD") and then, in direct opposition to the Wisdom of GOD in the Mystery, *Mr. Irving* sets up

---

*Irving* taught of this " Alpha and Omega of Theology," until these three or four years past? Surely his " ORATIONS" must be *full* of the Doctrine in question! Or, upon his own shewing, they are *empty things indeed,* as not setting forth " the Orthodox Faith."—*Mr. Irving* himself is shewn to be but " a Novice," even in his own Creed—and we need not wonder at the great Ignorance of the *People* " in these most ignorant days," since *they* have only been so very recently instructed in the A. B. C. of their Theology by their *Minister!*

Reader! " Consider what I say; and the LORD give thee understanding in all things."                                                    2 *Tim.* ii. 7.

* As this appears to be one of the principal grounds on which *Mr. Irving,* in his " Orthodox Doctrine," builds so many false conclusions having the most ruinous consequences, I purpose noticing this subject more at large, together with his delusive notions on those important Doctrines of Regeneration, Holiness, Righteousness, Atonement, &c. in some of the subsequent Notes, if not in a Postscript designed to accompany this Letter.

his own Reason—which can no more help him to the conclusion of Faith, than the Virgin's reasoning could have led her
to the knowledge *how* a *Virgin* should conceive, and a *Virgin*
bring forth a Son! all things being possible to Him who believeth, while none of these things are possible to him who
merely reasoneth. For what doth *Mr. Irving?* He stum-
bles "at that stumbling-stone"—the *Person* of "THE LORD'S
CHRIST,"* who is the only "Foundation laid in *Zion;*" since
he makes the *Divine Nature* of CHRIST to be the *whole Person* of CHRIST (whenever any personal Acts are spoken of in
reference to His people) and not the *two Natures*, the Human
and the Divine, so united as to constitute but *one Person*—for
the *Person* of "the LORD'S CHRIST," as spoken of in *Luke* i.
is not simple, but complex—not merely one *Nature*, but *two*
perfect *Natures* united in the one Person of IMMANUEL, GOD
WITH US"—the *Human* Nature (both Soul and Body) being
as necessary as the *Divine*, to constitute Him " The CHRIST
OF GOD"—" GOD manifest in the Flesh"—the Anointed of
the LORD—the Mediator, Surety, Saviour and Redeemer of
His People. But *Mr. Irving separates* the two *Natures*, instead of particularizing, or distinguishing them, and thus
destroys the complex *Person.* I pray you, my honoured
Friend, to mark *this* attentively, that *Mr. Irving separates*
the two *Natures* in CHRIST, (even in the face of his own
Church *con*fession, and his occasional *pro*fession to the contrary), and sets up *one* only (the GODHEAD) as the *Person;*

---

* " Drunken with Delusion and the cup of Error," as *Mr. Irving* says of
himself in the last page of his " Orthodox Doctrine," he has therein given us
some quotations from his Sermons, in which his " unsober fancy" " forms her
imaginations (airy shapes!") both of GOD and of Godliness, " through Philosophy and vain deceit, after the Traditions of men, after the Rudiments of the
World, and not after CHRIST!" Hence *Mr. Irving's* unbridled Spirit has amongst
other things, set before us in the above Work, a TWO-fold GODHEAD in the
LORD JESUS CHRIST—a *three*-fold NATURE in his COMPLEX PERSON—and a
*fourth* " SUBSISTENCE" in the undivided Essence of GOD! These " *high* Points of
Truth and Reason," which *Mr. Irving* says " he is continually straining his faculties to express;" (and of which he may well exclaim, as he does, " LABOR
INGRATUS:"—145.) together with the *numerous* CHRISTS he has set forth in
the above Work, and each ONE a *false* CHRIST—with the delusive Statements
he has made concerning the WORK of CHRIST, and also the WORK of the HOLY
GHOST, with other important Subjects, it is my intention to notice more particularly in some of the subsequent Remarks appended by way of Notes to this
Letter, or in the intended Postscript, should some Circumstances, not at present
within the limits of my control, allow the same to appear.

and, in so doing, he exhibits a CHRIST that is not "the LORD's"—that is not GOD-MAN—and " that CANNOT *save.*" Inasmuch as the GODHEAD of CHRIST was *essentially holy,* *Mr. Irving* asserts that CHRIST was holy; what time he avows, elsewhere, that one part of Him (His Human Nature) was *inherently sinful!* Observe his words on page 421: he there says, " I believe that MY LORD did come down, and toil and sweat, and travail, in exceeding great sorrow, IN this Mass of Iniquity with which I and every sinful man are oppressed ;" and " that *this* was HIS great work of humiliation and suffering !"

Here he speaks of " His LORD," when he evidently means His *Divine* Nature only—and this Divine Nature of CHRIST, by *Itself,* is evidently what he there improperly calls " his LORD." Who, he says, he believes " came down,"—and this *Divine* Nature he believes did " *toil*"—and this *Divine* Nature he believes did " *sweat*"—and this *Divine* Nature he believes did " *travail*"—and that too, IN a " Mass of Iniquity"—or, in his own words elsewhere used, " IN a Human Nature in which was *inherent* every variety of Human Wickedness!" Hence, therefore, it is evident, that this *He,* (the *Person* who *came)* is necessarily confined by *Mr. Irving* to the *Divine Nature* of CHRIST, which is only *one part* of His *Person* —and all those Acts that are mentioned, such as toiling, sweating, travailing, &c. are all attributed *to* that very *Divine* Nature *acting* IN the *Human* Nature\*— the whole of

---

\* And thus *Mr. Irving* thinks he may vilify the *Human* Nature of the LORD JESUS CHRIST, to any extent his " unsober fancy" may lead his " unbridled Spirit," without affecting, in the smallest possible degree, the *Holiness* of our LORD's *Person:* although he informs us in one place, that " He is one *Person* IN two natures," p. 87 ; and in another, that " His WHOLE Person consisted OF *both* natures, Human and Divine !" 85, 86. While in the quotation following, which is but one out of many that might be adduced in proof of his incessant contradictions of himself, and on fundamental points, *Mr. Irving* evidently excludes the Humanity from forming any part of the PERSON of CHRIST, (in *his* view at least) and therefore thinks he may, with the greatest impunity, assert the total depravity of " *That* HOLY THING," which is expressly declared to have been " OF the HOLY GHOST," and to have been " conceived" (or " begotten" as *Mr. Parkhurst* renders it) IN " the Virgin, by the overshadowing of the HOLY GHOST," *Matt.* i. 18, 20. *Luke* i. 35. " For certain, (he says) CHRIST had a Body and Soul of Man's substance, without thereby having a *Human* PERSON : and THEREFORE *we can* ASSERT *the* SINFULNESS *of the* WHOLE, *the* COMPLETE, *the* PERFECT HUMAN NATURE, *which He took, without in the least implicating* HIM *with* SIN." *Orthodox Doctrine,* Pref. x.

which actings are impossibilities, according to *Mr. Irving's* own shewing on p. 442, 3; for *there* he says, " I *utterly deny* that any thing suffered but the *Human* Nature of CHRIST; and *that* according to the measure of a *Man!*" Whereas, in the quotations given above, he expressly declares he *believes* that it was " his LORD" (the *Divine* Nature being so called by him) " who came down," " and toiled," " and sweat," " and *travailed*" " IN this Mass of Iniquity"—and that *this* was His (i. e. CHRIST'S) *great* Work of *humiliation* and *suffering.*" And thus *Mr. Irving* utterly *denies* in one page, what in another he declares he *believes.* And no marvel that he should deny his *own* Faith, after he has denied the *inherent holiness* of the great *Object* of Faith; and has said of other Persons, (by how much his superiors in the knowledge of the Truth another day will shew,) that they are " given up of God to believe *a Lie;*" because, forsooth, they will not believe with him in his " handling the Word of GOD deceitfully," as he does, when he makes this perilous addition thereto, that " CHRIST came in SINFUL *Flesh!*"*

Again: on p. 431, *Mr. Irving* says, " HE was the *Holy Thing* born"—and " HE was presented without spot unto GOD upon the Cross." " It doth not make HIM a Sinner that HE took *sinful Flesh,* any more than that HE came INTO a *sinful World,* and departed INTO *Death.*" " *I say* HE took sin-*ful* Flesh, and yet was sin-*less.*" In all these statements *Mr. Irving* evidently speaks of the GODHEAD of CHRIST, and *that only,* as constituting the PERSON of CHRIST:—and so, because *His* GODHEAD was *holy,* he asserts, (in substance) that *it* could not be *sinful!* whereas *Mr. Irving's* CHRIST evidently consisted of a *Divine* Nature, a *Sinful Body,* and

---

* It is " noted in the Scriptures of Truth," that " Every word of GOD is *pure.*"—" ADD *thou* NOT unto His Words, lest He reprove thee, and Thou be found a Liar." Prov. xxx. 5, 6. " For I testify unto every man that heareth the words of the prophecy of this Book, If any man shall ADD unto these things, GOD shall add unto him the plagues that are written in this Book." Rev. xxii. 18.

*Mr. Irving* tells us that he is " accustomed to tremble before GOD's word," (p. 126.) and so he well may after his truly perilous Additions to it, and false Interpretations of it, and the many fearful and horrible things he has uttered against the Inherent Holiness of " The SON OF MAN," as recorded in that 126th page of his " Orthodox Doctrine." *No Arian,* or *Socinian,* I believe, has ever yet dared to assert what is there set forth concerning the Human Nature of the LORD JESUS CHRIST; and which, if things are to be called by their proper names, must, I consider, be denominated, a Devilish description of GOD's " HOLY CHILD JESUS!"

a *Sinful Soul.* But, my honoured Friend, was it indeed the GODHEAD of CHRIST that was *born* of the Virgin? That which *really was* born of the Virgin, you know, is called a "Thing," (*Luke* i. 35.)—a Thing "*conceived*"—" a Thing *conceived in,* or *within* a *Creature,* and itself a Creature—conceived " *of* the *Holy Ghost*"—a *Holy* Thing conceived *of* the HOLY GHOST, *in* a *Virgin*—and which Holy Thing *existed not* until the overshadowing of the HOLY GHOST:—all which expressions, and many others, such as "a new thing created in the earth"—"GOD's Son made of a Woman," &c. directly oppose the supposition that it was the GODHEAD which was "*that* HOLY THING"—or that it was the GODHEAD that was "born."* It is true that we read in *Luke* i. 35.

---

* In order to reconcile the apparent contradiction between two capital "points of Orthodox Doctrine—(as *Mr. Irving* justly calls them) that the SON OF GOD was conceived in the womb of the Virgin and born of her, yet without Sin,"—"and yet that the GODHEAD cannot suffer," or become passable, &c. *Mr. Irving* has invented a " Subsistence"—as *he* calls it—which is, I believe, a something entirely *new;* and of which *I* may say, what he does of the supposed pre-existent Human *Soul* of CHRIST, that "it is a gratuitous Hypothesis; a filmy something, a celestial essence of Humanity, *between* the GODHEAD and the vile Substance of the Virgin : so that while there was an appearance of one thing to us, there might be the reality of another thing to Him." (p. 57.)

From *Mr. Irving's* own statements in pages 143, 144, it now appears, that it was *not* the *essential* GODHEAD of the SON that became incarnate, but some "Being," or " Subsistence," which he calls " *Christhood,*" (and by some other terms,) but which evidently exhibits an *inferior God;* which " none of his Fathers knew," and which is utterly unknown in the Scriptures of Truth. To this fancied " Being," *Mr. Irving* appears to assign the same place and period of existence, as are given by other persons to the supposed pre-existent Human *Soul* of CHRIST : and for the same purpose—namely, in order to bring within the grasp of *natural Reason* those " things of the SPIRIT OF GOD" which must be received altogether " through the Faith of the operation of GOD," or not at all. Now, this " Being" which *Mr. Irving* calls " *Christhood,*" he also informs us was " a Subsistence" which " the Persons of the GODHEAD set up among themselves, before the "World was;"—which " was, in the *origin* of its existence, inseparably united and made eternally one with the Second Person of the glorious GODHEAD :" and, thus united, he calls *this Complex* Object, " *Christ*"—" the *Word*"—" the *Logos*"—" GODHEAD subsisting in an *intelligible Form* in the Person of the SON"— and by other terms I have not room to particularize here—(see pp. 143, 144, 145.) To this " *Christhood*" he expressly ascribes a " *Godhead;*" and the various terms he uses by which to shew its *inferiority* to the essential GODHEAD of the SON, at once manifest the absurdity and prove the non-entity of this *inferior Deity,* which his own fancy has made. For he expressly tells us that this *Christhood* possessed " a *limited Godhead*"—" a glorious *Fulness* of Godhead, *not absolute,* but contained"—a *Godhead* that was " not incomprehensible," but " an intelligible *Godhead*"—" all *within the bounds of pure Reason !*" (144, 145) and many such things he asserts of it, which shew its inferiority to JEHOVAH ; such as its being passable, changeable, conveyable,

that "*that* Holy Thing" which should be born of the Virgin should be *called* "The Son of God"—but there is another word in the Text, which, being attentively considered, clearly shews that what was born of the Virgin was *not* the *Divine* but the *Human* Nature of the Lord Jesus Christ—"therefore also *that* Holy Thing"—or "therefore that Holy Thing also, which shall be born of thee shall be called the Son of God :" the name of the *uncreated* Nature being also given to that which was *created*, because of the union of the latter to the former in the one complex Person of Christ, God-man.

Here then *Mr. Irving* must maintain that, that which was "born of the Holy Ghost was the *Divine* Nature, or the *inherent holiness* of the *Human* Nature of Christ must be admitted from this very Scripture. I know, indeed, that *Mr. Irving* has spoken (p. 440) of the Godhead of Christ being "contracted," "self-contracted," so that "*He* doth condescend *out* of the Godhead *into* the bounds and condition of fallen manhood"—(by which unscriptural phraseology I suppose he means, that the *Divine* Nature of Christ became so compressed as to dwell *in* the *Human*,) but this is only another lamentable instance of *Mr. Irving's* mental speculation in the things of God ; in setting up *his Reason*, and

---

and created.—The whole of which unite to prove, that the very terms *Mr. Irving* has applied to the object of others' worship, may the rather be applied to this *Christhood* of his own :—namely, that it is "a notion of man's Invention," (117)—"a *God* constructed for Himself," (103)—"a *God* made in the Schools of Theology," (142)—"the *God* of the natural man," (103)—"A *God* of *Fictions*, a *God* of *variableness*, a *God* of *make-believes*, and *not* of *Truths*." (117.)

Of this "*Christhood*," thus united to the *essential* Godhead or Divine Person of the Son "before the world was," *Mr. Irving* says, in page 144, "Now contemplate the Son of God *thus* subsisting as *The Christ* before Creation, and you have *The Being* which was made Flesh and dwelt among us ;" which died upon the accursed tree," &c. "His Godhead all the while remaining unchanged, His *Christhood* alone passeth through the condition of humiliation and death." Thus, by setting up the Creature of his own "unsober fancy," (coming down, as this Christhood evidently does, out of that "high region," or "sphere of thought and reasoning," wherein, *Mr. Irving* informs us, he is continually straining his faculties to express "those high points of Truth and *Reason*," and "up into which," for their souls' good, he must drag those "who are not accustomed to think in that region,") he evidently denies the Mystery of "God with us," and destroys the Incarnation of the Son of God altogether ! Since he tells us that the *Mystery* of "How God could be born, crucified, suffer, and die," &c. *is to be* reconciled *by* the Doctrine concerning *The Christ* delivered above, *and in no other way whatever*." For, "from the point at which *The Christ* is set up, and God in the Person of the Son becomes active in *Christ*, from *that point it* is all *intelligible*, all *within the bounds of* pure Reason!" (145.)

rejecting *Faith*, which alone can set him right.—Since in one page he speaks of the *Divine* Nature of CHRIST being *taken* by Him "OF the FATHER's Substance," (421)—in another, as receiving the HOLY GHOST, (441)—and in a third, "self-contracted" by His own Power! (440) "The Law and the Testimony," however, know nothing of the GODHEAD of CHRIST being either "taken of any one—or receiving the HOLY GHOST—or being contracted, or self-contracted," any more than they avow the Sinful nature of His Manhood; but *they* expressly declare that, "that HOLY THING also" which should be born of the Virgin, should be called the "SON OF GOD"—and that "in Him dwelleth ALL THE FULNESS of the GODHEAD *bodily!*" (*Col.* ii. 9.) This "HE," who was the "Holy Thing born," and the "HE" who was "presented without spot to GOD," *Mr. Irving's* Sentiments shew, was the *Divine Nature* of CHRIST, as much as the "HE," who, he says, "took sin-*ful* Flesh and yet was sin-*less*." And this appears to me to be the plain Exposition of His Great Mystery, "how the SON OF GOD took sin-*ful* Flesh, and yet was sin-LESS!" namely, That His GODHEAD *only* was His *Person*, which could not become sinful in itself, although (as *Mr. Irving* asserts) united to Sinful Flesh and Blood.

---

And he evidently destroys the *Incarnation*, because he makes the *inferior God-head*, or "*Christhood*," to have assumed Human Nature, and not the SON OF GOD. The following order, if observed, will shew at once how the *intervention* of *Mr. Irving's* "*Christhood*" opposes and destroys the Gospel Mystery of GOD *Incarnate*, or "GOD manifest in the Flesh:"

| THE SON OF GOD, | i. e. | "His *absolute Godhead*," | p. 144. |
| *The Christhood*, | | "His *limited Godhead*," | p. 144. |
| The Manhood. | | "His *sinful Human Nature*," Pref. x. |

The very same words which *Mr. Irving* uses as words of command to his Brethren "who are stirred up," as he expresses it, to do battle over *Men* for the Bulwarks of *Zion*—(in fact, to fight against the Truth of GOD,) "Attack it, expose it, root it out, destroy it; and let the last breath be a Testimony against it,"—will justify this attempt of mine to expose the deadly tendency of his Sentiments; and concerning which I would say, in the very language that he utters against some of the most precious Doctrines of the Grace of GOD, "I desire nothing less than the subversion of all such notions, Root and Branch," (103) —"Away with it, away with it from my Theology for ever:" (117)—"It is a pestilent Heresy," (54)—And, "I make no doubt in saying that the opposite Doctrine is damnable; that to believe it is to believe a Lie; to die in the Faith of it is to die in the Faith of a Lie: and like every Lie I believe it will work the glory of the Devil, who was a Liar from the beginning, and not the Glory of JESUS CHRIST, who is the Truth, nor the glory of the "FATHER, who is true; and in Him is no darkness at all." For we know that "*No Lie is of the Truth.*" *Orthodox Doctrine*, p. 141.

Again : in page 431, *Mr. Irving* says,

" *He* (the SON OF GOD) was a PERSON of ANOTHER *Family* ; a *Son* of ANOTHER *Father*. Who then shall charge HIM with Sin ; coming, as HE came, from the fountain Head of Divinity, where HE had a personal Subsistence in the light of Holiness for ever and ever? HE had no Sin when HE *came* INTO our Substance, to atone for, and HE gat none while HE was IN the Flesh : whence then should HE have it? Is it Sin for GOD to *come* in the *Person* of the SON INTO what *Estate* HE pleaseth? Is it Sin for HIM to overcome all Sin IN that *Estate?* What would they have more to make HIM SINLESS, than that when HE came HE should have NO *Sin*, and that when HE dwelt among us HE should *overcome* ALL Sin? '

In all these assertions, as well as in many others that follow, the *Divine* Nature of CHRIST is that alone to which *Mr. Irving* applies the pronoun " He :"—and thus he makes the GODHEAD only to BE every thing, and to DO every thing, instead of the GOD-MAN, or the Complex Person of CHRIST, consisting of two natures, the human in union with the divine. It is true that, on some occasions, where necessary to serve his purpose, *Mr. Irving* asserts that CHRIST is *one Person* IN *two natures*"—and yet, when any personal acts are spoken of as being performed by CHRIST, he makes but ONE *Nature* only (namely, the divine) to be the *Person* who *is* every thing, and who *does* every thing,—and this *Divine* Nature being holy, *Mr. Irving* asserts that CHRIST was holy—although he maintains at the same time that His *Human* Nature, was in itself, and of itself, " full of Sin," and a " Mass of Iniquity." Thus, dividing the natures, *Mr. Irving* virtually denies that the Humanity was any part of the *Person* of the GOD-MAN ; and, by unavoidable consequence, falls into the Error of supposing that the GODHEAD of CHRIST performed what is utterly incompatible with an infinite nature to perform ;—as *Mr. Irving* himself also shews, on another occasion, in page 443.*

---

* The very questionable shape in which *Mr. Irving* sometimes states his own views—the truly erroneous representations he has given of the views of others—and the equally false consequences he has drawn from both—can never be given in evidence in favour of that clear mental perception concerning each, which he would take to himself in pages 27, 28. In the latter, he states, " Now it seems to me, that the root of their error (that is, of those who hold the Sinlessness of the Human Nature of our LORD,) is in mistaking Christ's *Human Nature* for His *Person*, or supposing it to be *another Person*."—Whereas, his opponents no more suppose that the Human Nature alone was CHRIST'S *Person*, or that it was " *another Person*," than *Mr. Irving* does ; but they *do* maintain that the *Human* Nature of their LORD is as much a part of His *complex Person*

There are various other places where the same thing is stated by *Mr. Irving*, in other words—see p. 435, for instance: there he says,

" The *Person* of the WORD did take a *human Will* under *those very Bondages*," (" the oppression of the Devil, the World, and the Flesh,") " into union with *Himself*."—In p 440 he says, " The *only* PERSON *in* CHRIST is the *Person* of the SON OF GOD"—(that is, in other words, the *Divine Nature* of CHRIST is the *whole* of the *Person* of CHRIST) and this Divine Nature, " by the power of self-contraction," which *Mr. Irving* says, " belongeth not to a finite, but to an Infinite Being"—" condescends," as he phrases it, " *out of* the GODHEAD *into* the bounds and condition of fallen Manhood," (p. 440)—and this Divine Nature of CHRIST, so " self-contracted," which thus *condescended out* of the GODHEAD *into* the condition of *fallen Manhood*, (as *Mr. Irving* says) " *acted* unto the redemption of that Form of Creation, and all Creatures dependent upon it; to overcome the Sin which oppresseth it, to destroy the Potentate of Death, and to bring in an eternal Redemption of the Creation of GOD. HE, the *Person* who thus condescendeth, is the *same* as He was *before*—the SON of GOD," (440) —" *He* was a Holy One, in spite unholy Creation. GOD *comes* and *joins* HIMSELF to His *own* sunken, ruined Creation, and redeems it." (p. 441.)

Thus, here, as elsewhere, *Mr. Irving* makes Redemption (which he plainly states to be *universal*, 445) to consist in the mere *actings* of CHRIST's *Divine* Nature (which is *holy*) WITHIN His *Human* Nature—(which he declares to be still *sinful*); hence, in p. 443, he speaks of the " *coming* OUT" of the GODHEAD—or, as his own words are, " the coming out

---

as GOD-man, as is the *Divine;* and which *Mr. Irving* plainly denies in all the quotations given above; and in multitudes of others that might be produced. " The *only Person*, IN CHRIST," he says, (p. 29) is the *Person* of the SON OF GOD."—By which term he means to set forth the Divine Nature of CHRIST to the exclusion of His *Human* Nature in forming any part of His *Person*. And hence in the Preface to his " Orthodox Doctrine," (p. x.) he shews how fearlessly he can assert the entire Sinfulness of CHRIST's Body and Soul, without in the smallest degree implicating His *Person*. His words are these: " For certain CHRIST had a Body and Soul of man's Substance, without thereby having a *Human Person;* and THEREFORE *we can assert the* SINFULNESS of the *whole*, the *complete*, the *perfect* HUMAN NATURE, *which He took without in the least implicating* HIM *with Sin !*" It is *Mr. Irving*, therefore, who sets up an erroneous View of the *Person* of the LORD JESUS CHRIST, and not his Opponents; and on that Foundation of Sand he erects a Superstructure, which will no more stand the test of GOD's *Holy Word* in *this* day of His *Mercy*, than it will endure the Floods of His *Righteous Indignation* in *that* day of His *Wrath* when every *Babel* Building must fall, " And,

Like the *baseless fabric* of a vision,
Leave not a *Wreck* behind !" (*Isaiah* xxvi. 5.)

of the infinite plenitude and blessedness of the *Godhead to
DO*" *every act* of CHRIST. And that "Here is the infinite
meritoriousness of His actings, in taking to *Himself* a Body,
and IN that Body for ever acting." (443) And this is what
he elsewhere calls, "GOD's coming INTO what *Estate* He
pleaseth." (431) "The LORD's perilous work IN *Flesh*,"
(422) "For it is GOD who *doth* the thing." (444.)*

---

* Not dealing in "the things of the SPIRIT OF God"—which all the faithful
servants of the LORD have an experience of in their own Souls, by the "demonstration of the HOLY GHOST and with Power," and by which alone they become
acquainted with the Truth of GOD,—*Mr. Irving naturally* enough turns to "*his
own* things, not the things which are CHRIST's;" and these he expresses in his
own words, not "in the words which the HOLY GHOST teacheth:" just like some
*English* Painter, who, having never been out of his native land, yet pretending
to give us some of the most faithful Sketches of *Chinese* Scenery, clothes the
Trees with a Foliage so truly *European*, that every Traveller immediately detects
the imposition. Into this Error, by a certain sort of necessity, *Mr. Irving* has
fallen; for, the things of which he speaks, and whereof he sometimes so very
dogmatically affirms, not being "of GOD," he finds not in the Holy Scriptures
a Phraseology suited to express his own unscriptural and unholy views, and
therefore supplies his own. This he plainly discovers when speaking of those
two precious Doctrines that might be mentioned, amongst others, namely, the
*Atonement*, and *Redemption*. Of the *former*, he plainly shews he likes not the
*term:* (p. 89.) of the *latter*, that he dislikes the *thing:* and however he may
retain the *word* "Redemption," either on its own account or as a substitute for
that of Atonement, it is manifest that he brings no "*Thus*, and *Thus* saith the
LORD," in confirmation of *his statement* of the *Doctrines*. Indeed *Mr. Irving*
never pretends to inform us, as the Scriptures do, that the Gospel Redemption
is a Redemption by *Blood;* and *that* Blood "the *precious Blood* of CHRIST, as
of a Lamb without Blemish and without Spot"—(1 *Pet.* i. 19.)—that "CHRIST
hath redeemed us from the *Curse* of the *Law*, being *made* a *Curse for us*,"
(*Gal.* iii. 13.)—that "it is the *Blood* which maketh an Atonement for the Soul,"
(*Lev.* xvii. 11.)—And that "in *Him* we *have* Redemption *through His Blood*,
the forgiveness of Sins, according to the riches of his Grace," (*Eph.* i. 7.) But
*he* asserts what the Scriptures do *not*, namely, that Atonement and Redemption
are the *names* for the bearing of CHRIST's *Work upon the Sinner;* and have *no
respect* to its bearing upon the GODHEAD! (p. 99.) Now, (leaving for the
present all observation on the absurdity of a Redemption that hath no bearing
on the GODHEAD), would any one really suppose that *the Sinner* here mentioned
by *Mr. Irving* is the *Human Nature* of our LORD JESUS CHRIST! INTO which he
makes His GODHEAD first to *come*, and IN which he afterwards makes it to ACT,
(to use his own unscriptural terms) "unto the *Redemption* of that form of Creation and all Creatures dependent upon it!" And thus, *Mr. Irving* makes the GOD-
HEAD of *Christ* to redeem His OWN *Manhood;* as we see in the above expressions
concerning GOD's "coming *into* what Estate He pleaseth, and overcoming all Sin
*in* that Estate;" and GOD's coming and joining *Himself* to His own sunken, ruined
Creation, and *redeeming* IT." So also, in pa. 89, he repeats the above quotation,
that "the Person of *The Word* did take a Human Will under those very Bondages, (the oppression of the Devil, the World, and the Flesh,) into union with

Herein, my honoured Friend, *Mr. Irving* doth most egregiously err; namely, in making only *one* of the *two*

---

Himself; and *acting* THEREIN, did *deliver* IT completely out of those Oppressions." Which deliverance of a Will in bondage, he makes to be the Redemption: and then he says that, as " his Adversaries deny CHRIST's Will to have been a bond-Will, " what need had IT of Redemption? And how is CHRIST's Work IN Flesh a redemption of *our Will*, if so be His *Will* was not lying under our bondage? So in his Preface, (pa. x.) after having spoken of the Flesh of CHRIST as His whole Creature-part, and as distinguished from his *Person* (His *Flesh* being there described as *sinful*, but His *Person*, that is, His *Divine* Nature as *holy*) he calls Redemption " the wonderful work which *Christ* wrought IN *it*," (that is, in His *own Flesh*: for the *Christ* there working is evidently His *Divine Nature only*). Again; in pa. 2, we read, " I believe that my LORD did bring His *Divine Person* into Death-possessed Humanity, into the One Substance of Manhood created in *Adam*, and by the Fall brought into a state of resistance to, and alienation from GOD, of condemnation and proclivity to Evil, of subjection to the Devil." And thus *Mr. Irving*, not only in these, but in various other places, and in various ways, sets forth a *fancied* Redemption by CHRIST, through His *Divine* Nature vanquishing the World, the Flesh, and the Devil, *in* His own *Human* Nature: such *Human* Nature being made the Field of Contention in which this War is waged between the GODHEAD of CHRIST, one while, and the HOLY GHOST at another; (for both are sometimes mentioned) such *Divine* Nature being essentially *holy*, and the *Human*, so inherently *sinful*. Mark the following words on pa. 40., in proof of this statement: " The Flesh of CHRIST was the *middle space* ON which the powers of the World *contended* with the HOLY SPIRIT dwelling in His Soul. His Flesh is the *fit medium* between the powers of Darkness, and the powers of Light?" " And why fit? Because it is linked unto all material things *Devil-possessed*." " His *Flesh* is the *fit Field* of Contention, because it is the same on which *Satan* hath triumphed ever since the Fall." To which I must add those other words of *Mr. Irving's*, on pa. 13. " It is said GOD sent Him about Sin: Sin was the thing that brought Him. He came to put away Sin by the Sacrifice of Himself; and if for Sin, and nothing else but Sin, He came, where was He to find it but in our Flesh, where its Head-quarters are. Could he find it in *Adam's Flesh*, Oh ye *empty* ones? Would ye go above the Fall to look for Sin, Oh ye *idle* ones? He came about Sin, and nothing else; and where found He it? In *Flesh*, and no where else. For the *Devil*, great Sin-originator, had taken his position up in *Flesh*, and was to be defeated by Man, by whom he had thought to have defeated GOD."—" If *Devil*, if World, are to be overcome; if Sin is to be met at all, it must be met in *Flesh*. To seek it elsewhere is to seek to no purpose; to *fight* it elsewhere is to beat the Wind. As surely as you expect to find an Usurper at the head of his Army, or in his Strong-hold shut up, so must you expect to find Sin in *Flesh*. *Here* the *Devil* had wrought *his* Work; and to destroy the Works of the *Devil* the SON OF GOD was manifested."

Hence it appears, that *Mr. Irving's* Redemption is not a Redemption of *Persons*; neither is it a *particular* one; but rather of " a Nature," of an " Estate," or " Condition," of a "Region," which it is said CHRIST's GODHEAD came *into*; a *general* Redemption, or of *all Human Nature*; and of our LORD's Humanity also in the General Mass: for that being alike " inherently Sinful," alike " Sin-possessed," " Death-stricken," " Devil-minded," and " Devil-possessed"—as *Mr. Irving* describes it—stood in the *very same need* of the *very*

*Natures* in CHRIST to constitute the *Person* of CHRIST :—for although His *Human Nature* was not *a Person,* (considering that term to denote some intelligent or thinking Being that has Reason and Reflection *by itself,* which the Human Nature of CHRIST had not, it never having subsisted by itself or in any state separate or apart from His GODHEAD,) yet, from the very instant when " the WORD was made Flesh" in the womb of the Virgin, the *Person* of CHRIST, which, previous to such union had been from Eternity *simple,* or only *divine,* (although in GOD's All-seeing Eye it was *ever foreseen,* and *fore-ordained to be,* just what in the fulness of Time it was manifested to us,) actually became *complex,* that is, both Human *and* Divine—and GOD-MAN was the *Person:* the Human Nature, including both Soul and Body, being as much a part of the actual GOD-MAN, as the Divine. And ever after such union had taken place in the conception of the Virgin, whatever related to the *Human* Nature of CHRIST, either in Soul or Body, related to the PERSON of CHRIST, GOD-MAN; and whatever related to His *Divine* Nature, related to His PERSON as GOD-MAN. Whereas *Mr. Irving* evidently considers the PERSON of the GOD-MAN to be His *Divine Nature only!* and on that account I have quoted his words so largely, because of the momentous consequences of this Error; which

---

*same Redemption* that the *Lump* did—and, according to *Mr. Irving's* account it received it too ! And even THAT ONLY is *sometimes* made to be ALL that was redeemed ! ! 149. See also pp. 3, 4, 68, 80, 88, 89.

Hence it appears also, that *Mr. Irving's* Redemption is not a Redemption to GOD " by the Blood of His SON," the holy and the righteous Servant of the Father, as GOD-MAN; but it is a Conquest or Victory obtained by the *Divine* Nature of CHRIST warring against the World, the Flesh, and the Devil, inhabiting His *Human* Nature, during the whole of his Life, and even after His Death on the Cross, (p.127.) Just as we might suppose a Man, who, possessing a House infected with Leprosy, which was unlawfully occupied by Robbers, should come into it and contend with those Robbers, and bind them and imprison them therein, until the Leprous House should fall; so CHRIST's GODHEAD is made by *Mr. Irving* to come *into* his Sinful Manhood (a Leprous House indeed !) and *therein* to overcome the Devil, the World, and the Flesh, without producing any *change* in the Flesh from Sin to Holiness, until the Morning of the Resurrection; and the Sinful Human Nature of Christ forming no part of the *Person* of CHRIST, any more than the Leprous House did any part of the *Person* of the Man whose property it was, and who overcame his Enemies therein. *This* Redemption may be considered by *Mr. Irving* as one of those " high points of Truth and Reason which he is continually straining his faculties to express," —but, blessed be GOD! that " we have a more sure Word of Prophecy whereunto we do well to take heed, as unto a Light that shineth in a dark place." *2 Pet.* i. 19.

destroys at once both the Doctrine of Imputed Righteousness, as well as that of the Atonement; and deprives every truly awakened Sinner of the only ground of Hope set before him in the Gospel:—for, " if the Foundations be destroyed, what can the Righteous do ?" But, blessed be God ! both for the glorious Fact, and the personal spiritual knowledge of it— that " the Foundation of God standeth sure, having this Seal, The Lord knoweth them that are His." (2 *Tim.* ii. 19.)

And here I must most unequivocally maintain, that the *Sinfulness* of the Human Nature of the Lord Jesus Christ, destroys the doctrine of a Sinner's Justification before God through the imputed Righteousness of Christ; because it is impossible, on *Mr. Irving's* Scheme, that any Righteousness could have been wrought out by the *Christ* which *he* here sets forth; who is composed of essential God-head united to a " *fallen* Manhood;" (or in other words, to a *Sinful* Soul and a *Sinful* Body*).—For, in the first place,

---

* One of the most deadly effects of *Mr. Irving's* reasoning on the things of God, appears in the *numerous Christs* it has produced, and *each a false* one! Pre-eminent among the rest stands that One, which he designates " The *Christ;*" of which we read so many unscriptural things, in such unscriptural language, towards the close of " The *Orthodox* and *Catholic* Doctrine;" and to *which Christ* alone I shall confine my Observations in this Note; designing to notice the others in another place. This *Christ*, is evidently that of *Human Reason— not* of *Divine Revelation. Mr. Irving's Christ*, (as he himself calls Him, p. 64,) and *not " The* Christ of God." A *Christ*, which is at *one* time composed of *Two Natures*, and *both* of them *Divine* : namely, a *superior* and an *inferior* God-head ! At *another* time, made up of *Three Natures*, to wit, the *superior* God-head—the *inferior* one—and a *Sinful Manhood!* While at *another*, and in the more general way, but *one Nature* is exhibited as forming the *Person* of *Mr. Irving's Christ*—and that, the *superior Godhead* alone ! All these, I think, will appear in the following quotations, taken from a Work of indisputable authority " in these most ignorant times"—" The *Orthodox* and *Catholic* Doctrine of our Lord's Human Nature"—written by *Mr. Irving* for the express purpose of settling upon the " *one only Foundation* of the *Church*," the " insecure and unsteady Faith of almost all, in the *true* Humanity of Christ." (pp. 1, 142.)

1. In confirmation of the assertion that but *one* nature is frequently set forth by *Mr. Irving* as composing the *Person* of Christ, I must adduce the following, in addition to the foregoing quotations I have already given on that head: " I wish it to be steadily borne in mind in reading this Tract, that whenever I speak of the *Flesh* of Christ, I mean, except when the contrary is expressed, the *whole Creature-part*; which is not a *Person* but a *Substance;* a Substance which we must describe by its *properties* of sinfulness, and darkness, and deadness, in order to understand the wonderful work which Christ wrought *in* it. *What* was *holy*, was His Person; and from *that* came Redemption *into* the Nature: *What* was *powerful*, was the Person, and from *that* came *Strength*

there could not have been any real "delight in the Law of
GOD" within the Heart of *such* an one—neither could He

---

into the *Nature*." *(Pref.* x.) " The PERSON being the PERSON of the SON OF
GOD." (pa. 3.)   And His Humanity is called a " *Nature,"* apart from " HIM"
—the PERSON.—*Pref*. vii.

Herein *Mr. Irving* first shews that CHRIST's Flesh, (or " whole Creature-
part," as he terms it,) because it was *not* a *distinct Person* of itself, is therefore
*no part* of the *complex* Person of the LORD JESUS CHRIST;—" the *Person* being,"
he says, " the *Person* of the SON OF GOD :"—(by which he means His *Divine*
Nature only.)   Next he distinguishes between the two so as to *divide* them ; by
calling the GODHEAD of CHRIST the *Person,* and the *Humanity* into which that
*Person* came, the *Nature.*  He continues this distinction and division by noticing
their *properties,* or *qualities*—the *Person* (that is, the *Divine* Nature) he calls
*holy*—but the " Substance," (that is, the *Human* Nature) he calls " *Sinful.*" And
then he makes a further distinction and division as to *Act :* by saying, " what
was *holy* was the *Person,* (meaning the GODHEAD) and from *that* came *Redemption* into the *Nature,* (meaning the *Manhood*): what was *powerful* was the *Person;*
and from *that* came *Strength into* the *Nature.*"   Thus, the *Person* of CHRIST is
here represented as both *holy* and *strong :* while His *Manhood,* (*into* which *that
Person* is said to *come,*) is made to be both *sinful,* and *weak;* as it is both here,
and also elsewhere described, (72) ; and the *Redemption* which is here spoken
of as being brought *by* the *Person into* the *Nature,* is elsewhere set forth (and
has been before noticed) as the *Godhead* of CHRIST warring *in* His *Sinful Manhood* against the World, the Flesh, and the Devil, and at length by the Resurrection, but not before, overcoming them, and turning them all out! (See the
preceding Note, and *Cath. Doc.* pp. 13, 40, 67.)

2. In support of the declaration that *Mr. Irving* sometimes makes *his Christ*
to consist of *two* Natures—and *both* of them *divine*—the one, a *superior Godhead,*
and the other, a *Godhead* that is *inferior*—I refer to pages 143, 144, 145, of his
" Orthodox Doctrine :" in which he calls these two natures, (when united)—
" Christ"—" *The* Christ"—" The Word," or " Logos ;" and informs us that by
the name " *Christ*" is signified, *Godhead* subsisting under an *intelligible Form*
in the *Person* of the *Son ;* which " *intelligible Form*" we afterwards find was that
*inferior Godhead* which *Mr. Irving's* " unsober Fancy" has created; and which
he also distinguishes by the term of " *The Christhood* :" through the supposed
union of which " Christhood" to the *essential* GODHEAD of the SON, on the one
hand, and to His supposed " *sinful Manhood*" on the other, *Mr. Irving* thinks
to reconcile to his *Reason* HOW it can be said that the SON OF GOD was " born,"
was " crucified," " died," &c. and yet no change take place in the nature of
GOD.  For " *How* are they to be reconciled ?" he asks, p. 144.  " They *are* to be
reconciled," he replies, " by the Doctrine concerning *The Christ delivered above,*
and in *no other way whatever.*"   Which *Christ* he describes thus : " Before the
World was, the *Persons* of the GODHEAD set up among themselves *The Christ,*
as hath been said, and the SON (that is, the GODHEAD of CHRIST) took *that Form*
of Subsistence," (which he elsewhere calls " the *Christ-Form,*" and by which
he means what he terms the " limited *Godhead ;*" (p. 60, 144) and was GOD subsisting as *The Word,* the *Logos,* before the World was." (144.)  " Now contemplate the SON OF GOD thus subsisting as *The Christ* before Creation, (that is,
His *Divine* Nature in union with this " Subsistence," or *inferior Godhead*) and
you have the *Being* which was " made Flesh, and dwelt among us ; which died
upon the accursed tree," &c. which " Being," as it is called in p. 144 ; or

have " loved Righteousness and hated Iniquity," as we are
assured the LORD'S CHRIST did, *Heb.* i. 9.    And, in the

---

" Subsistence," as he terms it, on the same page, we are there informed " was
in the *origin* of its existence inseparably united and made *eternally one* with the
*Second Person* of the *glorious* GODHEAD :" and was " that *Holy* Thing conceived
of the Virgin : (CHRIST'S *Human* Nature being, as elsewhere called, the *sinful*
Thing.)   Now, " For nothing," he observes, " hath the Orthodox Church, in all
time so zealously contended, as to affirm, that GOD was born of a Virgin, and
that GOD died upon the Cross, &c. ' On the other hand, no point hath been
more diligently argued, and more explicitly pronounced in all ages of its existence, than this, That the GODHEAD cannot suffer, nor be tempted," &c. (p. 143.)
These " apparent contradictions," he says, " are to be reconciled in this way,
and in no other way whatever : GOD first realizes to Himself a Subsistence, as
the Word in the Person of the Son ;" (by which Subsistence he means " the
Being" which he calls " Christhood," which the Trinity " set up," or gave
existence to, before Time ; which being *then* united to the Godhead of the SON,
constituted the WORD) " and the SON *thus* subsisting, *not* in his *absolute* Godhead, but in his *limited* Godhead, becomes Flesh and becomes dead !" (144.)
    Here, then, we have the point proved by *Mr. Irving's* own words, that *his
Christ* possessed *two Godheads !* the one he expressly terms " His *absolute Godhead,*" and the other, " His *limited Godhead ! !*"   The *inferior* he has evidently
invented in order to gratify his own *Reason,* and get rid of the divine Mystery ;
which, though infinitely above *our* Reason, is, nevertheless, within the grasp of
God's Reason, and not at all mysterious to *Him.*   For, in the very next sentence to the above, in page 145, *Mr. Irving* goes on to state how he thinks he
has accomplished his object in setting up *two Godheads* in CHRIST—the one
" absolute," and the other " limited :" " His GODHEAD all the while remaining
*unchanged,* His *Christhood* ALONE passeth through the condition of humiliation
and death." (144.)   *How* this invention of *Mr. Irving's* destroys the Mystery
of the *Incarnation,* " GOD with us," has been already shewn in a previous Note
on pp. 24, 25, of this Letter.
    3. That *Mr. Irving* sometimes makes *his Christ* to consist of *three distinct
Natures*—namely, essential or absolute GODHEAD—his inferior or limited one—
and his sinful Manhood—I refer to those words before quoted, from p. 144,
" GOD first realizes to Himself a *Subsistence,* as the *Word* in the Person of the
SON ; and the SON thus subsisting, *not* in His *absolute Godhead,* but in His
*limited Godhead,* becomes *Flesh,* and becomes dead.   His GODHEAD all the
while remaining unchanged, His Christhood alone passeth through the condition of Humiliation and Death ; and yet the identity of the *Person* is preserved, whether you look to His subsistence in *Godhead* absolute, or His
subsistence in *Christhood* before the worlds, or His subsistence in *sinful Flesh.*"
*Mr. Irving's* own words here present us with—1st. the " *absolute Godhead* of
CHRIST, and that unchanged"—2nd. His " *limited Godhead, or Christhood,*"
which he says, " passed through the conditions of limitation and death"—and,
3rd. His *Flesh ;* and that, *sinful* Flesh !   Again, in page 145, he says, " Of the
SON OF GOD, then subsisting as *the Christ* within the bounds of Reason and of
Word, it is said in the text that he became dead."   By this " SON OF GOD" is
here meant the Divine Nature of CHRIST, or his true and essential GODHEAD :
by " the *Christ* within the bounds of Reason and of Word," is meant that fancied " Subsistence" which he calls " Christhood," the " Godhead *not* absolute

D

next place, as there could not have been any such *Delight* in
the Law of God in His *Heart*, so there could not have been
any acceptable *Obedience* in His *Life;* for the Flesh and
Spirit of CHRIST, *Mr. Irving* says, were, of their own nature,
both sinful, and so remained even to the last; no change
having passed upon either of them anterior to the Resurrection. (422.)    The Law of God (the perfect Rule of
Righteousness) requires perfect *Holiness* in the *Nature*, as
well as perfect *Conformity* in the *Life* of every one who is
made under it; for " the Law is holy, and the Commandment
is holy, and just, and good." (*Rom.* vii. 12.)  But CHRIST, as
it respects his *created* Nature, *Mr. Irving* says, was " Sinful," " Corrupt," and " Evil;"—" Every variety of Human
Wickedness being inherent in His Humanity."  *No Obedience,* therefore, could possibly have been rendered by Him,
even for *Himself*, (which even *He* must have needed,) and
much less on account of others, He being so inherently sinful
—yea, so pre-eminently wicked! And as it was not possible
for the *uncreated* Nature, or GODHEAD, (which *Mr. Irving*
here makes to be the *Person*) to be made *under* the Law, or
to have yielded the least Obedience required of the *Human*

---

but limited," &c. and which he tells us the " *Persons* in the TRINITY set up
before all Worlds," and then united to the Person of the SON; and by His
becoming " dead," is meant, the assumption of a sinful Manhood by the *inferior Godhead* or " Christhood," (as his term is) and in which Manhood such
*Christhood* is said to have suffered and died!

Again; in page 146, he says, " When, therefore, it is said, *Christ* became
*Flesh*, it is signified that *He* who heretofore had subsisted in the *glory* and *fulness* of *Godhead intelligible*, did empty Himself thereof, and come into the conditions and limits, and passions and affections of *Manhood*, such as Manhood is
experienced by us to be, such as Manhood is by GOD defined to be." Here, also,
we find the three natures before noticed; the " He," who is here referred to, set
forth the *essential* GODHEAD of CHRIST—The " *glory* and *fulness* of the *Godhead
intelligible*," (in which that *He* is said to have heretofore existed) shew the
*inferior Godhead* or *Christhood;*—and the " Manhood as experienced by us to
be," is designed to exhibit CHRIST's Human Nature in all respects as *sinful*
as ours; or, as it is elsewhere called, His " fallen Manhood."

And thus, with marvellous inconsistency, after all his boast of superiority
in making the matter " all intelligible," " all within the bounds of pure Reason,
*and which to know is life eternal*," (145.) *Mr. Irving* makes the matter just as
unreasonable as it is unscriptural; and which, if relied upon as the ground of
Hope, will certainly issue in ETERNAL DEATH: *Mr. Irving* here making *his*
Christ to consist of *three distinct natures* – a *superior Godhead*, an *inferior Godhead*, and a *sinful Soul and Body* in all respects like ours! And while in this
place we find him " setting up" an *inferior Godhead*, after his own fancy—in

Race, (for the GODHEAD of CHRIST was certainly *above* the Law of the Creature,) so neither was it the *essential* Righteousness of the Divine Nature that was *required*, but the actual Obedience of the Sinner's Substitute, " GOD'S HOLY CHILD JESUS," (very GOD-MAN) in Thought, Word, and Deed. For, as it was not GOD Himself, but His holy *Creature* MAN, that first sinned in the Person of the *first Adam;* so it was not GOD, but the one only *Mediator* between GOD and Man, the MAN CHRIST JESUS, the " HOLY ONE OF GOD," " the *Second Adam*, who went to the end of the Law for Righteousness to every one that believeth." But there could have been no Righteousness whatever *wrought out* by the LORD JESUS CHRIST for His People, on *Mr. Irving's* Hypothesis, nor does he ever pretend to shew that there was, either by CHRIST'S *Divine* Nature, or by His *Human* Nature, or by *both* in *union;* because His Manhood being " Sinful," (as *Mr. Irving* says) must have marred the whole; since it is absolutely impossible for any Creature to *be inherently sinful* and yet *act righteously* as the Law requires. Of course, no Righteousness could have been *brought in, placed* to His People's account, or *put upon* them; ever has been, or *ever*

others we detect him in doing away with even the ESSENTIAL GODHEAD *itself!* even the Divine Nature of the FATHER, of the SON, and of the HOLY GHOST also !! For he tells us the FATHER "emptied *Himself* of GODHEAD," which was " *poured out* UPON the SON—the HOLY GHOST *conveyed* the INFINITE GODHEAD INTO the SON—and the SON not only emptied *Himself* of His own " GODHEAD *Properties*" as the SON, but of what He had received as the *Christhood* also. And thus this GODHEAD-EMPTYING system of *Mr. Irving's*, at last leaves NOTHING even of the *unchangeable* JEHOVAH, in *existence!* And of course there could be nothing of it in the *Person of his Christ:* for the *Godhead Person Mr. Irving* speaks of as coming " *without* GODHEAD PROPERTIES," is as great an absurdity in Theology, as it would be in Nature to talk of the Sun's shining upon us at noon-day, without either light, or heat, or any influence in its beams !

In this way *Mr. Irving* makes it manifest to those to whom " the LORD has given eyes to see, and ears to hear, and hearts to understand the things of the SPIRIT" by the teaching of the SPIRIT, that, instead of " going into the plain and fruitful Field" of Holy Scripture, in order " to gather Herbs for the Saints' Family meal," he has wandered into the Mazes of Error and Confusion, which he describes as a " high sphere of Thought and Reasoning," (131) the Things of which (" those high points of Truth and Reason,") he is " continually straining his faculties to express;" (145) but in which he has evidently found a " *wild Vine*," and gathered thereof *wild Gourds* a *Book full!* These he has " shred into the pottage," which, when brought to that test of fire which is to " try every man's work of what sort it is," is shewn to be so baneful, that the true Children cannot eat thereof, but are constrained to cry out, each one to his fellow, " there is DEATH IN THE POT, *O Man of* GOD !" 2 *Kings* iv. 38—40.

*will be!* And although *Mr. Irving* once *asserts,* that *his
Christ did* " work out an *everlasting* and *universal* Righteousness,*" (441) yet *he* only asserts *that,* just as he does
many other things which he cannot prove ; for he does not
inform us that *this* Righteousness (wrought out by *his sinful
Christ,* and so universal in its extent as he would have it to
be,) was the GOD-MAN'S Obedience to the holy Law of GOD, in
Thought, Word, and Deed, in order thus to magnify the Law
which we had thus broken ;—but that it was some new and
unheard of thing throughout all Holy Scripture, namely, *His*
" OVERCOMING *universal* TEMPTATION, and *for ever destroying the* TEMPTERS !!*" (441.) This statement may probably
satisfy *Mr. Irving's* mind, and the minds of all such other
persons as " say they are rich, and increased with Goods, and
have need of nothing, and know not that they are wretched,
and miserable, and poor, and blind, and naked," as lost and
ruined Sinners in the sight of GOD's holy Law ; but *such a*
description of RIGHTEOUSNESS is not only a very *Vanity*
before GOD, but must ever be an *Abomination* in His Sight ;
is no where to be found in the Scriptures of GOD ; nor can it
ever really satisfy the enlightened conscience of any *truly
awakened* child of GOD, who is taught by the SPIRIT of GOD
to know that " Sin is the transgression of the Law," and
that the " Righteousness which delivereth from Death" as
the just penalty of the Law, is the perfect Obedience unto
Death of that " HOLY ONE OF GOD," that " ONE MEDIATOR
between GOD and Man, the MAN CHRIST JESUS."

Again : in pa. 441, *Mr. Irving* states, " that the *Person* of the SON
OF GOD took a reasonable Soul and corruptible Flesh joined together
after the constitution of a man, as men are found to subsist : HE, the *Person* of the SON OF GOD, for His condescension to take that Soul, and
*therein* to honour His Father, did receive the HOLY GHOST; which ever
receiving and ever using, He did sustain His Human Will against the Law
of the Flesh in its largest and most comprehensive activity ; and presented
fallen Human Nature subdued unto Holiness, made obedient to the
Law of GOD ; presented His Creature Will, sustained against all visible,
sensible oppositions, in perfect harmony with the Will of GOD. And is
*this all ?* THIS IS ALL !!!"

Here, my honourable Friend, we have another description both of Holiness and of Righteousness, which the Scriptures of Truth know nothing about ; for, had they contained
the *Doctrine Mr. Irving* avows, they would doubtless have

afforded him *Terms* in which to have expressed it; and he would have readily directed us to the chapter and to the verse wherein the same Doctrine was to be found: for the *Truths* of GOD are always much better expressed in the very *Words* of GOD than they ever have been, or ever can be, in the *Ashdod Phraseology* of worldly-wise men, however learned or polite.* Now, from the above quotation it appears, that the

---

* How striking is the difference between the writings of *Mr. Irving*, and those of the Prophets and Apostles, in this particular also! *They* delighted to set forth the " things of GOD" in the very words of the SPIRIT of GOD; whereas *Mr. Irving* takes pleasure in exhibiting *his own Things*, in a *Phraseology* that is altogether his own; and which, to " the Church of the living GOD, the Pillar and ground of the Truth," is not only a dead letter, but an " unknown tongue."

*Ezekiel*, when commissioned *of* the LORD to go to the rebellious house of *Israel*, was commanded *by* the LORD to speak *His* words unto them; as we read in *Ezek.* ii. 7. " whether they would hear, or whether they would forbear." So again in *Ezek.* iii. 4. " Son of man, go, get thee unto the house of *Israel*, and *speak with* MY WORDS unto them." And the Apostle *Paul* not only assures us that when *he* came among the people *he* came among them " not with excellency of speech declaring unto them the *Testimony* of GOD;" and that " *his* word and *his* preaching was *not* with the *enticing Words* of *Man's Wisdom*, but in Demonstration of the SPIRIT and of Power"—but he also enjoins on all Preachers, " If any man speak let him speak as of the *Oracles* of GOD:" even as the Apostle himself did when he said, " which things also we speak, *not* in the *Words* which *Man's* Wisdom teacheth, but which the HOLY GHOST teacheth," 1 *Cor.* ii. 13. Let the *real* Believer in our LORD JESUS CHRIST take up any single page of *Mr. Irving's* " Orthodox and Catholic Doctrine," or any two or three in succession, (say for instance, pages 143, 4, 5.) and carefully compare them with " the Oracles of God," and he will not only find the same couched in *unscriptural Language*, but exhibiting the most *unscriptural Things*. For who has ever yet met (between the first verse in the Book of *Genesis*, and the last in that of the *Revelation* by *John*,) with any such *Terms*, any such *Persons*, any such *Things*, as the following: " The *Christhood*"—the " *Godhead* absolute," and " the *Godhead not* absolute" in CHRIST—" the *Godhead* limited," and " the Godhead *not* limited," in CHRIST—" His Subsistence in *Christhood* before the Worlds"—" the *Christ*-form of being"—" the *Word*, not in His *absolute Godhead* but in his limited *Godhead*, becomes Flesh"—having " a glory fulness of *Godhead not absolute*, but contained"—" the Person of the SON in coming into Manhood must not bring with him GODHEAD *Properties*, though He bring with Him a *Godhead Person*." And all this " intelligible," " all within the bounds of pure Reason, from that point in which *the Christ* is set up:"—or in plain terms, from some period in *Eternity*, in which *Mr. Irving* has presumed that an *inferior* or *created Godhead* was brought into existence, and united to the *superior* or *absolute Godhead* of the LORD JESUS CHRIST!

*Mr. Irving* may rank these things among those " high points of Truth and Reason" which are to be known only in that " high region of Thought and of Reason," in which he says " ye idle ones!" " ye ignorant ones!" are " not accustomed to think," and " up into which he must drag us, for our soul's

GODHEAD of CHRIST received the SPIRIT, or HOLY GHOST ;*
(for it is the *Divine Nature* only that is meant by the word
" *He,*") and so receiving it *continually,* His GODHEAD did
sustain His *Human Will* by *Power* against His *sinful Flesh;*
or, as it is elsewhere called, " the Law of the Flesh in its
largest and most comprehensive activity," (that is, in plain
Language, the Law of the Flesh, which is the Law of Sin

---

good;"—and *Mr. Irving's* Friends, with him, may be sporting themselves with
these their own deceivings, under the delusive notion of possessing something
very superior, or " so very *Intellectual,*" as some have said—but the day is fast
approaching, when they will assuredly know, that what they now call " *Intellectual*" is *not* " that which is *Spiritual,*" in the sight of GOD. *Satan* still lies in
wait to deceive, hard by the *Tree of Knowledge;* by the fruit of which, as " a
Tree to be designed to make wise," he often succeeds with those whom " fleshly
lusts" might probably assail in vain ! A sort of Christianity which is *Intellectual* but *not Spiritual,* (or, in other words, the knowledge of the head through
*human learning* without the experience of the " new heart," under *divine teaching)* has long been the very body, soul, and spirit—and therein the great *bane*
of some Churches, of the members of which even Truth in the language of
Poetry might say,

" All Heart they live, all *Head,* all *Eye,* all *Ear,*
*All* INTELLECT, *all* SENSE !"

Yet unrepealed in Heaven's high Record, stands *this* carnal-intellect-con-
founding Truth :—" *Verily, verily,* I say unto thee, Except a man be born
again, he *cannot* SEE the Kingdom of GOD !" " *Verily, verily,* I say unto thee,
Except a man be born of Water and of the Spirit, he *cannot* ENTER INTO the
Kingdom of GOD !" *John* iii. 5. " For the *natural man* receiveth not the *Things
of the* SPIRIT OF GOD : for they are *foolishness* unto him : neither CAN he know
them, *because they* are *spiritually* discerned," 1 *Cor.* ii. 14.

* Elsewhere in his " *Orthodox* and Catholic Doctrine," *Mr. Irving* has
informed us, that it is the Office of the HOLY GHOST, First, to *unite the invisible
Godhead* with the *visible* SON ; and Secondly, to *furnish* the SON for the work
of bringing *Human Nature* into perfect reconciliation with, and obedience of,
GOD. (p. 120.) In the same page we are told, that the " HOLY GHOST doth *convey
the infinite* GODHEAD *into* the SON !" In another, that the SON " serveth HIM-
SELF with HOLY GHOST Power," (118.) In another, that the GODHEAD of the
FATHER was " *emptied out* upon" GOD the SON, (116, 155.) That " the *Person*
who could thus *bear* to have *emptied out upon Him* the fulness of GODHEAD's
various affections, (or, who could " *bear* GOD, or *sustain* the FATHER," as it
is in p. 118) could be no less than GOD, the SON of the FATHER !"—while " the
*Person* towards whom He *manifested* the *Ocean-fulness* of His *Being,*" the FA-
THER, " found in His *own* GODHEAD—the Person of His *own* SON !" (115.) In
another place we read of " the *Holy Unction* with which the FATHER supplied
His *believing* SON, and which the *obedient* SON ever used to RE-*strain* and CON-
strain the *Creature Substance*" (His " *sinful Manhood !*") " unto the Will of the
GODHEAD." (20.) In another place we are given to understand, that CHRIST
was both GEN-crated, and RE-generated, by the HOLY GHOST.(137.) In another,
that " CHRIST's Flesh had the GRACE of SINFULNESS and *Incorruption* from the

and Death, in its most *rampant* condition!) all the Lustings of which Flesh were " to do evil," and evil only, and that continually ! And this *Mr. Irving* calls " fallen Human Nature *subdued* unto *Holiness,* and made obedient unto the Law of God ! !" Although there was every " variety of Human Wickedness inherent in His Humanity, and His Mind or Soul being just as sinful as His Body, was not sub-

---

Indwelling of the HOLY GHOST, who prepared that Body out of the Virgin's Substance." (53.) In another, that He came into all the sin-*less* conditions of sin-*ful* Man. (104.) " Into the *very conditions* of the sinner." (117.) And that *His Faith* was " *not* that of a fault-*less* Man, *but* of an *infirm* and SINFUL *Man,* SUCH AS ALL MEN ARE." (105.) [*Query,* Whether such expressions as these may not serve to *explain* to *Mr. Irving's* Friends, at least, HOW " that *Holy Thing*" which was born of the Virgin, which *Mr. Irving* informs us was not only *gen*-erated but *re*-generated also of the HOLY GHOST, nevertheless had " *every variety of Human Wickedness inherent in the Humanity,* from the In-carnation to the Resurrection!" (17.) To know and to understand HOW " the SON of GOD took *sin*-FUL Flesh and yet was *sin*-LESS," being " the Alpha and the Omega, the beginning and the ending of *Mr. Irving's Orthodox* Theology."] In another place we are informed, that " CHRIST's Human Nature was such as we find it every where else; and a HOLY-GHOST Life in it, which the SON continually useth, and *acteth* UNTO *the Regeneration of it* after the Image of GOD in Righteousness and true Holiness."(120.) In another, that " from His con-ception, every *acting* of CHRIST's *mind* was *holy,* and every *acting* also of His *Flesh;* but this *not* in its *proper nature,* but through the *constraining* and *enforcing power* of His *Person,* ACTING GODHEAD BY THE HOLY GHOST."(23) And in ano-ther, that " by the Three-fold acting of the TRINITY, was *the* CHRIST consti-tuted a DIVINE and HUMAN NATURE! (53.) Herein we have *Mr. Irving's* own words setting forth that very " AMALGAM, or *mixture of Natures,*" which he so falsely charges upon, and so severely reprehends in, others. (p. 119.) For by the three-fold acting of the Trinity, *Mr. Irving's Christ,* be it observed is con-stituted *not one Person,* but—ONE NATURE! And when we consider also, that this *Human* Nature is declared to be *inherently sinful,* and that the *Divine* is *Infinitely Holy,* we have " confusion worse confounded," in the supposed one-ness or unity of things so diametrically opposite. And the ETERNAL *sinfulness* of this *amalgamated* NATURE, is also set before us; for *this Christ,* thus consti-tuted a *Divine* and *Human Nature, Mr. Irving* also declares was thus " joined in *personal union for ever !*"

After all the above contradictory, unscriptural, and absurd notions of the GODHEAD of the FATHER being " emptied out OF" *Himself*—" emptied out UPON the SON"—" the SON's serving Himself with HOLY GHOST POWER"—" the IN-FINITE GODHEAD *conveyed* by the HOLY GHOST *into* GOD the SON"—" GOD the SON *bearing* GOD the FATHER"—" GOD the FATHER finding in His *own* GODHEAD the PERSON of His *own* SON"—" the *Person* of the SON *acting* GODHEAD by the HOLY GHOST"—" and the *Trinity* constituting CHRIST a Divine and Human *Nature* for ever !"—We are told, that the Person of the SON OF GOD, " in ful-filling the *great work* of *bringing* the FULNESS of the GODHEAD into a *Body,* of manifesting GOD in the Flesh"—or " of coming into Manhood"—" *must not bring* with Him GODHEAD PROPERTIES, though He bring with Him a GODHEAD

ject to the Law of God, neither indeed could be." Having elsewhere informed us (p. 441.) that CHRIST's Soul was a " *fallen* Soul," and His Flesh " *fallen* Flesh," and both *fallen* " even to the last," and that " no change passed on either anterior to the Resurrection," (422) all this *subjection* to Holiness, all this " Obedience to the Law," of which *Mr. Irving* here speaks, can be no better, (to say the very best of it,) than the *Power* of GOD *preventing* the *sinful Soul* and *sinful Body* of CHRIST from bringing forth outward " Fruit unto Death;" (to which *Mr. Irving* maintains they were both inherently and incessantly inclined,) or the *Divine* Nature mortifying the sinfulness of the *Human* Nature, *in* the *Person* of CHRIST ! Which makes CHRIST to be divided against Himself ; and *if* CHRIST be so divided against Himself, " how then can *His Kingdom* stand ?" Where, then, is the HOLINESS *Mr. Irving* has spoken of ? Or whence came the RIGHTEOUSNESS, the " everlasting Righteousness," which he has once, and I believe but once mentioned, on pa. 441 ? since the " *fallen Manhood*" of CHRIST, whenever weighed in the holy and just Balance of the Sanctuary, must be found wanting of every thing Righteous, of every thing Holy ; and neither the Holiness or Righteousness of the *Divine* Nature is imputed to the Church, but the Obedience of " the HOLY ONE of ISRAEL," as the true GOD-MAN.

---

PERSON !" (118.) And that by a power of *Self-contraction* belonging only to a *Divine Person*, the SON OF GOD doth condescend *out* of the GODHEAD *into* the *bounds* and condition of *fallen Manhood !*" (29.) For what purpose, then, does *Mr. Irving* make the SON to be even TREBLY *Divine ?* Possessing, as he does, 1. His own Personal GODHEAD as the SON ; 2. That of the FATHER, which *Mr. Irving* makes to be POURED OUT UPON Him ; and 3. That of the HOLY GHOST— or what *Mr. Irving* calls " the INFINITE GODHEAD *conveyed* INTO the SON, by the HOLY GHOST." Thus annihilating the FATHER and the HOLY GHOST by this divesture or " emptying out" of the Divine Nature, and then again divesting or emptying the SON of His *own* Divine Nature, (as well as that of the FATHER said to have been " poured out upon" Him, and that of the HOLY GHOST, or the *infinite* GODHEAD said to have been " conveyed into" Him,) by the declarations that the *Person* of the SON in coming *into* Manhood must, by a *Power of Self-contraction, come out* of the GODHEAD, and must *not* bring with Him GODHEAD *Properties*, though He bring with Him a GODHEAD *Person !*" (118.) In this way *Mr. Irving* would make, not only Faith and the Holy Scriptures bow down to his vain Reasonings, but even all the Divine *Persons* in the glorious GODHEAD also ! " Bow down REVELATION, *vain Reason* reigns *here*," being no inapplicable motto, in my esteem at least, to the whole of the before-mentioned pages, if not to every other page, of the " *Orthodox* and *Catholic*

In many places *Mr. Irving* makes very positive Assertions, which are as contradictory of others made by him elsewhere, as they are opposed to the uniform testimony of the Scriptures of Truth. He informs us, in some places, that the "*Soul*" of CHRIST was "sinful"—"inherently sinful"—and His "*Body* sinful" also, and "even to the last;" but, that *all* the ACTINGS of His *sinful Body*, and of His *sinful Soul* were HOLY! This, I think, is making the *Tree corrupt*, and the *Fruit good!* At all events, it is declaring that "a *corrupt* Tree" *can* and *does* "bring forth *good Fruit*," in direct contradiction to those words of our LORD in *Matt.* vii. 18. But the *actings* of CHRIST'S sinful Nature, *Mr. Irving* says, were all *holy*, (what time he makes His *Flesh* to have "carried up to His Mind every form of Seduction" (426, 427,) and His *Soul* to have "held Communion with" all Wickedness in Wicked Men!) and that these pretended *holy Actings* of CHRIST'S *sinful Nature*, were *holy*, not through any *delight* there was in His *Heart* "to *do* the will of GOD," as from any *inherent Holiness there*, (for, in truth, the Heart of CHRIST, if sinful, must of necessity have *hated* both GOD, and GOD's *Law*—*Mr. Irving* himself having declared that it was "*at variance*," and even at "*enmity* with GOD," 434,) but that those Actings were holy, through a *Power* superior to His Human Nature, *compelling*, as by mere force, both His Mind and His

---

Doctrine of our LORD's Human Nature." For to what end have we the beforementioned unscriptural expressions concerning the advent of the SON of GOD —and especially of His coming *as a Divine* PERSON *without* Divine *Properties?* Is it not to make way for that Invention of *Mr. Irving's* vain Imagination before noticed, on page 144, called "the *Christhood*," or the *inferior Godhead* he has set up? If the SON of GOD really came into Manhood *without* GODHEAD PROPERTIES, then HE *never had* GODHEAD PROPERTIES; and *He* was *not* GOD who came! it being as great an absurdity to speak of a *Divine* PERSON's coming into Manhood *without Divine* PROPERTIES, as to speak of the SON of GOD's coming *without* HIMSELF! All the PROPERTIES of the GODHEAD being those Infinite Perfections of the Divine Nature without which GOD is not. *Immutability* is as much the very nature of GOD, as *Infinity* and *Eternity;* for it is His own declaration of Himself, "I AM JEHOVAH; *I change not*," *Mal.* iii. 6. The pride of carnal Reason has ever been the bane of Man! *Gen.* iii. 1, 6. However, "Let GOD be true, and every man a Liar." "And without controversy great is the *Mystery* of Godliness; GOD was manifest in the Flesh," 1 *Tim.* iii. 16. "Beware, therefore, lest any man spoil you through *Philosophy* and vain deceit, after the Tradition of Men, after the Rudiments of the World, and not after CHRIST. For *in* HIM DWELLETH ALL THE FULNESS OF THE GODHEAD BODILY." *Col.* ii. 8, 9.

Flesh to do Acts directly contrary to their own proper Natures; both Mind and Flesh being *sinful* from the very first moment of their existence in the Virgin, until the last instant of His Flesh being in the Tomb!\* Thus, the force of Omnipotence is represented as making the *Mind* of CHRIST *act* directly *contrary* to its inherent desires; and the *Flesh* of CHRIST is by the same Power, made to act likewise. And these *forced Actings* of the *sinful Mind* and of the *sinful Flesh* of CHRIST, *Mr. Irving* calls "HOLINESS," and "RIGHTEOUSNESS"!! But alas! how false! how awfully false are *Mr. Irving's* Views! how dreadfully delusive are *Mr. Irving's* Statements, upon these all-important Subjects! since they are directly opposed to those gracious Declarations of the SPIRIT of TRUTH, wherein

---

\* Of all such persons as may be opposed to the foregoing Exposition of *Mr. Irving's* views, making as he does the sinful *Human* Nature of *his Christ* to *act* directly contrary to its own inherent Properties or Qualities, through the compulsory power of the *Divine*, I would intreat an attentive consideration of the following plain but important Enquiries; the first of which, let it be remembered, is only made to introduce the objections contained in the other two.

*First*, has not *Mr. Irving* plainly declared, that there were *two distinct Wills* in the Person of CHRIST, considered as possessing *two Natures*, the Human and the Divine? The *Second;* has he not evidently stated, that the two Wills in the *Christ he* sets forth, were, in their own proper Natures or Qualities, as contrary to each other as any two Wills can be: the one being Holy, in all respects like the divine will of the FATHER; the other sinful, in all respects like the human will of His fallen Creature, Man? The *Third:* has not *Mr. Irving* most unequivocally asserted, that there was not the smallest possible *change* from *Sinfulness* to *Holiness* effected in the *sinful Manhood* of *his Christ;* but that the *properties* or *qualities* both of His Soul and Body were alike sinful, until the morning of the Resurrection? If so; then in the very face of all *Mr. Irving's* conclusions to the contrary, the two Wills in *his Christ* were no more in *Harmony* during His tabernacling on earth, than *Sin* is harmonious with *Holiness*, or the will of GOD is harmonious with that of *Satan!* And, recollecting here, that other important Declaration of *Mr. Irving's*, that the Doctrine of the *Atonement* " would be *distinctly*, and *flatly* denied, avoided, and *destroyed*," if these two Wills in the one Person of CHRIST were at any time INharmonious with each other, (pa. 63.) I turn to *Mr. Irving's* own words, in various places used, in order to prove that all the objections contained in the last two Enquiries are, by him, most unequivocally maintained.

1. The introductory Enquiry sets forth, that there were two *distinct* Wills in the Person of CHRIST; " the one the absolute Will of the GODHEAD," the other, " the limited Will of the Manhood," which, *Mr. Irving* says, (in p. 54.) the Church hath ever maintained as resolutely as that there were two Natures." In pa. 45, " Those who say there is but *one* Will in CHRIST, either make him only GOD, or only Man. There is the absolute Will of the GODHEAD, and there is the limited Will of the Creature. These two may be *consentaneous* with one another, which is *Holiness*: or they may be *dissentient* from one another, which

we are assured that "the LORD's CHRIST" "*delighted* to do the Will of GOD;" yea, that "GOD's Law was within His Heart:" whereas, the Heart of CHRIST, if inherently sinful, must have shewn that the *Law* of GOD was *not* therein; and that such Law His sinful Heart *must* have *hated,* but could not have loved, or have *delighted* in; and "the Law of Sin and Death" must have been that which actuated his Sinful Humanity. In the delight of the Heart of CHRIST to do the Will of God, we have the cordial spring of that true and perfect Obedience of our heavenly Lover and LORD, which afterwards flowed forth in all His Thoughts, Words, and Works; but, in *Mr. Irving's* representations, we have the unwilling drudgery of the most abject Slave—since it could no more

---

is *unholiness* in the Creature. But the *one* cannot be *the other*, without confounding two most opposite things, the Creator and the Creature."

2. That the two distinct Wills in *Mr. Irving's Christ* were *not harmonious,* but *contrary* to each other, as any two Wills can be: His *Divine* Will being *holy,* as the Father's; His *Human,* sinful, as our's. He says, in pa. 70, " The two things which had to be brought at one, were these,—the Will of Human Nature, and the Will of GOD, which, since the Fall, had been *ever* at *variance.*" In pa. 132, " the Man fell in his highest, noblest part, in his proper personality; and Sin entered into his *Mind,* into his *Flesh,* into Creation thereupon. They became *Sin-possessed, Devil-minded, Death-stricken.*" In pa. 126, " Manhood after the fall broke out into Sins of every name and aggravation; corrupt *to the very Heart's Core,* and from the *centre* of its inmost *Will* sending forth streams black as Hell. *This* is the human nature which *every man* is clothed upon withal, *which* THE SON OF MAN *was clothed upon withal, bristling thick and strong with Sin like the Hairs upon the Porcupine.*" In pa. 87, " If thy question, being rendered into Orthodox Language, be, Did He redeem the *Human Will* from the *bondage* of a *Nature* which drew it away from GOD, and was of *itself rebellious against* GOD? I answer thee, Yea, verily; *this was* WHAT *He did;* and THIS was the WHOLE of What HE *did* IN Flesh." So in pa. 54, " The work achieved by the GODHEAD, through the Incarnation of CHRIST, was *neither more nor less* than *this,* to bring the *Will* of the Creature, which had *erred* from the *Divine Will,* back again *to be harmonious* with the Divine Will, and *there* to fix it for ever." In pa. 89, " The Person of the Word did take a *Human Will* under those very Bondages, (the oppression of the Devil, the World, and the Flesh) into union with Himself." " The adversaries of the Truth agree with us, that the Will of Man hath to be redeemed out of the Bondage of the Devil, World, and Flesh; and they agree that to effect this the SON OF GOD took a Human Will; but they deny that this Will was a *Bond-will.* And what need, then, had *it* of Redemption? And how is CHRIST's work in Flesh a Redemption of *our* Will, if so be *His* Will was not lying under *our* Bondage? Or how is it a *Redemption* at all *?*" "Whatever use GOD may make of CHRIST's work, it is manifest that this work is *no work of Redemption,* if the *Will* He took was *not* a *Will* in *Bondage?*" In pa. 88, " If *His* Human Nature *differed,* by *however little,* from ours, in its *alienation* and *guiltiness,* then the work of reducing it into eternal harmony with GOD hath no bearing whateve upon *our Nature,* with

have been in the *Mind* of CHRIST, if sinful, nor in His *sinful Flesh*, to yield the smallest possible Obedience to any one Precept to the holy Law of GOD, than it is in the heart of the greatest Reprobate to do so:—and by how much *Mr. Irving* makes the Human Nature of CHRIST to have been *pre-eminently sinful*, or *inherently wicked*, in that very degree does he make the Obedience, the *pretended* Obedience of such an one, to have been *pre-eminently slavish*; it being produced by the energy of Almighty Power, *forcing* the *Enmity* of the Human Will, to the performance of those very Acts it *hated* even while it performed them; *Mr. Irving* having so repeatedly assured us, that there was not the smallest possible change in either the Body or Soul of CHRIST

---

which it is not the same." "And as to his having an *unfallen* nature to bring into oneness or reconciliation, the thing is *nonsensical;* for an *unfallen* nature, a *Will* in the state of Creation, is at *no Variance* nor *Enmity with* GOD, but His own good and pleasant workmanship." In pa. 41, "All His Life long the *Will* of the *Flesh* had been *successfully withstood* by the *Will* of the *Spirit*." And in pages 22, 23. "*Certainly*, there was *a Will* in Him which He contradistinguisheth from the *Will* of the FATHER; and which, I say, was the Will of the Flesh; *which in itself* is CONTRARY *to the Will of the* FATHER." "And in the face of all these certainties, if a man will say, that *His* Flesh was *not sinful Flesh as ours is*, with the *same Dispositions* and *Propensities* and *Wants* and Afflictions, then, I say, GOD hath sent that Man strong delusion, that he should believe a Lie."

3. That there was no *change* from sinfulness to Holiness in the sinful Manhood of *Mr. Irving's Christ*, but that the *Properties* or *Qualities* both of His Soul and Body were alike sinful *until the morning of the Resurrection*. In *Pref.* pa. vii. he says, "Whenever I attribute *sinful Properties* and *Dispositions* and Inclinations to our LORD's *Human* Nature, I am speaking of it considered as *apart* from HIM, in itself; I am *defining* the *Qualities* of *that* NATURE which *He took upon* HIM, and demonstrating *it* to be the *very same* in *Substance* with that which *we* possess." In pa. 7, "The constitution of *His* Human Nature was as the constitution of *our* Human Nature in *all respects*, and in *all conditions*." In page 20, "If a thing must be named by those *Properties*, which it *ever hath* in *itself*, and not from those which it derives from another thing most widely different and distinct from itself, then must CHRIST's Flesh be called Sin-FUL, and not Sin-LESS." In pa. 3, "CHRIST's *Substance after His generation* of the HOLY GHOST was the same as before, very Substance of His Mother, without change or alteration,"—"the *very Substance* which *fell* in *Adam*." (108.) "*Every variety* of human *Wickedness*, which hath ever been realized, *inherent* in the *Humanity*." In pa. 22, 23, "Certainly there was a *Will* in *Him* which *He contradistinguisheth* from the *Will* of the FATHER; and which, *I say*, was the *Will* of the *Flesh*; and which *in itself* is CONTRARY to the Will of the FATHER." In pa. 80, "As to His having an *un*-fallen Nature to bring into oneness or reconciliation, the thing is *nonsensical;* for an *un*-fallen *Nature*, a *Will* in the state of Creation, is at no *Variance* nor *Enmity* with GOD, but His own good and pleasant workmanship." In pa. 41, "All his Life long the *Will* of

anterior to the Resurrection; but that both were " fallen,"
" sinful," &c. and that even to the very last! And yet
*Mr. Irving* hesitates not to call these compulsory Acts of
CHRIST's sinful Nature, by the gracious and glorious terms
of " HOLINESS" and " Righteousness!" But if we have no
*other* " *Holiness*," if we possess no *other* " *Righteousness*,"
in which to stand before GOD, than these wild, unscriptural,
and delusive representations *Mr. Irving* has given of both,
*we* shall be found amongst those who are " clothed with
strange Apparel"—who *are* " covered with a Covering, but
*not* of MY SPIRIT, saith the LORD," in the day when " He
shall come to make up His Jewels;" and then " good were
it for us that we had never been born !" For, " if the blind
lead the blind, *both* shall fall into the ditch," *Matt*. xv. 14.

---

the *Flesh* had been successfully *withstood* by the *Will* of the *Spirit*. In pa. 37,
" In such a reasonable soul, (as all other men's) liable to Temptations through
the Flesh, and in such a Flesh (as all other men's) *loving* the TEMPTATION, and
*ever conversing* with the TEMPTER, (*Mr. Irving* asserts that the *Athanasian* Creed
declares, when it is himself only who avows) that CHRIST subsisted." In pa. 18,
" There is not a hint in all Scripture of any *change* that passed upon CHRIST's
*Flesh* in its Conception, or at any other time *anterior to the Resurrection*, so as
that it should *not* be Flesh of *our* Flesh—*Flesh* of the *same kind* with that of the
Brethren." In *Pref.* vii. " We maintain that it underwent *no change*, but was full
of Fellowship and Community with *us all His Life long*, and was *not changed* but
*by the Resurrection*." In pa. 78, " We deny that the mere *taking* of our Nature
*changed* it in *any* thing; we deny that the *bearing* of IT *about* with HIM *changed*
it in any thing; we deny that it WAS *changed before* the *Resurrection*." And in
pp. 127, 8, *Mr. Irving* says, " I believe it to be *most Orthodox*, and of the Substance and Essence of the Orthodox Faith, to hold that CHRIST could say *until*
His *Resurrection*, Not I, but *Sin* that tempteth ME *in my Flesh;* just as *after* the
Resurrection He could say, " I am separate from sinners." " And, moreover,
I believe that the *only* difference between His Body of Humiliation and His
Body of Resurrection is *in this very thing*, that SIN *inhered in the Human
Nature, making it mortal and corruptible, till that very time that* HE *rose from
the dead:* AND IF THIS PRINCIPLE MUST GO TO THE WALL, I SHALL GO TO THE
WALL ALONG WITH IT."

After all these positive assertions that the Will of the *Divine* Nature of *Mr.
Irving's Christ* was a *holy* Will, and that of his *Human* Nature a *Sinful* one,—a
Will in *Bondage*—a Will at *variance* with GOD—of itself *rebellious* against GOD—
at *Enmity* with GOD—*contrary* to the will of the FATHER—from its *inmost centre*
sending forth streams black as Hell—and which underwent *no change* from Sin
to Holiness all His Life long, until the Resurrection—After all these positive
assertions by *Mr. Irving*, and many similar ones that might be quoted, we find
him declare, pa. 70, " If CHRIST's *Human* Nature contradicted his *Divine*,
He is a *Sinner !*" But to assert which, He says, is Blasphemy, and therefore
he multiplies contradiction by absurdity in telling us on pa. 54, that " with all
this *he holds* the *human* Will of CHRIST to have been *perfectly Holy!* and to

In page 425, (where *Mr. Irving* is speaking of Sin) he says, " If the *Will consent not*, though the *Flesh be inclined*, there is *no Sin*. CHRIST's Will endured these Temptations exactly as mine doth ; He was tempted in all points like as I am ; but He yielded not to the Temptations, and was *therefore without* Sin." " But in all these instances (the Temptations in the Wilderness) His Will, never consenting, abode in its Integrity and Righteousness." " He never consented unto the Evil, but always preferred the good ; and by the *Power of His Will* constrained Tongue, Hand, Foot, Eye, Ear, and every Member, to do the very Will of GOD." (426.) " Though the Flesh of CHRIST was in all points liable to Temptation, as our Flesh is, and did carry up to the Mind every form of Seduction ; yet left it there no Sediment of Evil, no Taint of Pollution ; yet found it there no Response, no Inclination, but Abhorrence and Detestation of the deepest, powerfullest kind." (427.) " There was, therefore, no Concupiscence, no Thought or Meditation of Evil, no In-dwelling of Lust, no abiding of Anger, or Malice or Hatred ; but all was holy, lovely, beautiful, and perfect, as the Will of God ; and from that purest Fountain of Light, Life and Love, came forth

---

have *acted*, spoken, or wished nothing but in perfect harmony with the Will of the GODHEAD." In one page (89) he declares, that if CHRIST's Will were not a Will in *Bondage*, there could be no *Redemption*." But in another, (63) if it were ever *inharmonious* with the Divine Will, the Atonement would be " flatly denied." In one page, (88) he states, that if CHRIST's Human Will were not *at variance* with GOD, it were not *our* Will ;" but in another, (46) that if it *were dissentient*, that is *unholiness*; and then CHRIST is a *Sinner*. (70) In one page, (63) that His Human Will was *ever harmonious* with the Divine Will ; but in another, (41) that it was, all His Life long, successfully *withstood* by the Will of the SPIRIT : which effectually *resisted* " the *evil Propensity* of the fallen Man." (63.) In one page, (88) that CHRIST's work was that of reducing, or of bringing His *Human* Will, into oneness with the *Divine* Will, or " into eternal Harmony with GOD;" but in another, (63) that such Will was *ever harmonious* with the Divine Will ; while in a third, (41) this work was not accomplished *before* the Resurrection !

On what ground then, it may be asked, does *Mr. Irving* pretend that the *sinful* Human *Will of his Christ*, with all the *actings* of his *fallen Manhood*, can be considered *holy* in the sight of GOD ? I answer, on *this very delusive one*, namely, that the *Power* of the *Divine* Nature (which he sometimes makes to be that of the SON, and at other times that of the HOLY GHOST,) dwelling in the *sinful Human* Nature, without changing its Sinfulness into Holiness, REStrained continually the *fallen Manhood* from committing any outward *Acts* of Sin, and as continually CONstrained such *fallen* Manhood to perform other Acts which *Mr. Irving* calls *Holiness* and *Righteousness !*—or, as he terms the same, *restraining* and *constraining* the *Creature-substance*" (CHRIST's *Sinful Manhood !*) " unto the Will of the GODHEAD." (20) Both the Body and Soul of *his Christ* being just as *inherently Sinful* when *on the Cross*, as he asserts they were in the Womb of the Virgin, and all His Life long, until they were *altogether changed* in the *Resurrection*. (66.) And although he speaks of CHRIST's being presented on the Cross " *holy* and *without spot*," &c. *Mr. Irving* never means by any such expressions that the Human Nature of CHRIST was then *inherently* SINLESS, but that the same had merely been preserved from any

evermore Streams of Divine Goodness, Righteousness, and Truth. *Every Member* of His *Body* HE *constrained* to obey the great Behests of GOD. HE took the *Prey* out of the *Hands* of the Mighty. HE gave *Satan no Lodgment* or *Residence;* HE gave *Sin no Quarters within* HIS BEING." (427.)\*

In the foregoing Quotations attempts are made to prove, that CHRIST was righteous, and holy, because it is there said that CHRIST's *Will* did not *consent* to Sin; but since *Mr. Irving* sometimes speaks of *one* Will in CHRIST which refers to His *divine* Nature—a *Second,* which relates to His *Soul*

---

*outward Acts* of Sin, through the Power of GOD; or " the energizing of the HOLY GHOST," as he terms it; (pa. 132,) and that " CHRIST did so *endure* its *Vileness, withstand* its *Sinfulness, restrain* its *Propensities,* and present it free from an UNHOLY ACTION upon the Cross." (38.) Now, the attentive Reader will observe, that this freedom from any *unholy* ACTION on the Cross, is pretended by *Mr. Irving* what time he there makes the Humanity, in itself, to be *full* of " *Vileness,*" " *Sinfulness,*" and " *Propensities*" of " *the fallen Man!*" (38, 63.) And this presentation of CHRIST's *inherently sinful Body and Soul on the Cross,* (after they had been kept from *outward Acts* of Sin during all His Life, by the Power of GOD restraining the evil Propensities of both) *Mr. Irving* elsewhere calls CHRIST's " *sustaining* His *Human* Will *against* the *Law* of the *Flesh,* in its *largest* and *most comprehensive activity,* and *presenting* FALLEN HUMAN NATURE SUBDUED UNTO HOLINESS, MADE OBEDIENT TO THE LAW OF GOD! (30.) which term " *made,*" he evidently considers, (pa. 136,) as a *Compulsion* or *Force against* the *Will,* and *not* the *voluntary Choice* of the Person acting. And hence, speaking of this *delusive Holiness* which he attributes to the LORD JESUS CHRIST, he also says, " Now, from His Conception every ACTING of His mind was *Holy,* and every ACTING also of His Flesh; but *this* NOT IN ITS PROPER NATURE," (that is not inherently, or by its choice) " but *through* the CONSTRAINING *and* ENFORCING POWER of His *Person,* ACTING GODHEAD, by the HOLY GHOST!" (p.23.) " Yea, verily, he adds, (on pa. 111,) He (CHRIST) knew the *evil Law* of that Nature He was clothed with;" (and which Nature *Mr. Irving* informs us, on pa. 126, "*from the centre of its inmost Will sent forth streams black as Hell!*) " He knew *every point* and *passage* of it, and *at* every point and passage of it He *met* it with the SPIRIT, and *drave* it *back,* and *put bonds upon* it, and *led* it *forth again tamed* and *reclaimed;* a *Servant,* of *itself* an UNWILLING Servant, and still *in all things* a Servant unto GOD!"

Not to enlarge here upon the open violence *Mr. Irving* has done to the Rule, that " The Will cannot be constrained;" it is evident, on comparing the statements he has made in order to support the *Counterfeit* HOLINESS and RIGHTEOUSNESS of his *Sinful Christ* on the Cross, that he has " flatly denied, avoided, and destroyed" the no less *Counterfeit* ATONEMENT he has elsewhere set up (pa. 63,) in his fancied Reconciliation and perfect Harmony between those two irreconcileable and inharmonious things—the *holy Divine* Will, and the *sinful Human* Will, in the Person of *his Christ.* And therein *Mr. Irving* has not only opposed his own Sentiment, but " condemns Himself in the very thing that he allows."

\* So exceedingly delusive, and so extensively destructive is the Error, that the *Divine Nature only* of the LORD's CHRIST constituted the *Person* of CHRIST, that its " Desolations wide, and vast, and wild," meet us almost in every Page and a *Third*, which regards His *Body*, (and which last he calls the *Will* of His *Flesh*,) he ought to have particularized *which* Will he meant when speaking here of *His* Will "not consenting to Sin." Having in other parts of his production so repeatedly and so pointedly represented both the Soul and Body of CHRIST as "*sinful*," "*inherently* sinful," and *both so* "*sinful* to the last"—and having set forth the GOD-HEAD of CHRIST (inhabiting His "*fallen Manhood*") as His *Person*, one would have thought that *Mr. Irving* necessarily meant the Will of CHRIST's *divine* Nature, when he says, that *His* Will "yielded not"—"never consented"—"*He* never consented to the evil, but always preferred the good: and by the power of *His* Will constrained Tongue, &c., and

---

of the Book opposed by these Notes. Viewing this subject as the "radiating point of Error," I may be allowed here, as well as in other places, to expose that truly Sandy Foundation on which *Mr. Irving* erects his Superstructure of Error, to the rejection of the only Foundation laid in *Zion*, and revealed in the Scriptures of Truth."

It is evident that the *Human* Nature of the LORD's CHRIST either really *did* constitute a part of the *Person* of CHRIST, or it *did not*. Deny that it *did*, and of necessity you deny, not only that CHRIST's *Person* was *Complex*, but "the great Mystery of Godliness, GOD manifest in the Flesh;" and deny at the same time the possibility of any *Personal* Obedience having been rendered by the *Second Adam* for the *Personal* Transgressions of any of the Children of the *First*; since the *Divine* Nature of CHRIST could no more obey the *Requirement* of the Law, on their account, than it could suffer, bleed, or die, in the endurance of its *Curse*, for the same Persons. It was a *Person* that sinned in the *first Adam*, but a *Nature only*, (and that no part of the *Person*) which *Mr. Irving* makes to be obedient, in the *Second !*

Deny the *inherent Holiness* of the *Human Nature* (admitting *that* to form a part of CHRIST's Complex Person,) and you necessarily make CHRIST to be *a Sinner !* Sin being, as *Mr. Irving* himself says, on pa. 38, "Any want of conformity to, or transgression of, the Law of GOD;" and "No act of CHRIST being the act of *either Nature*, but of the *Person*, including *both* Natures." (70.) And, thus making CHRIST to be a Sinner, you stand justly accused of Blasphemy, (even by *Mr. Irving* himself, pa. 2.) and at once, and for ever destroy the only ground of the believing Sinner's Hope—the BLOOD AND RIGHTEOUSNESS OF HIS INCARNATE GOD ! For, the Blood of a *Creature*, so *inherently sinful* as *Mr. Irving* makes CHRIST's Humanity to have been, instead of being *inestimably precious*, must have been *transcendantly vile;* and instead of *Itself cleansing* the Believer from *all* Sin, *Itself* needed to be *cleansed from every Sin !* since "every variety of Human Wickedness," it is asserted, was inherent in the Humanity !! And to affirm, that any acceptable *obedience* for *others*, could be wrought out by one who had such an inherently *sinful* Nature *Himself*, would be as absurd as to speak of the Righteousness of the *fallen* race of *Adam* being wrought out for the Justification of *fallen Angels*, or the Acts of *Fallen Angels* justifying *them!*

all *His* members to do the very Will of God"—for, in pa. 435, he declares that CHRIST's *Human* Will was a "Bond-will"—(and, of course, *sinful,* since His Soul is said to be inherently so) and the Will of His *Flesh,* he says, was in itself "*contrary* to the Will of the FATHER"—(424) and of its *own proper nature inclined* to *do all* the *Works* of the *Flesh*—(426) and that *it* was a Will at *Enmity* against GOD (434) and under all our Bondages to the Devil, the World, and the Flesh!—the Human Nature of CHRIST differing "nothing from our's in its alienation and guiltiness!"—(434). Now the above assertion cannot be true, that "the Will of CHRIST" did not *consent* to the Evil, but abode in its Integrity," if His *Human* Will be intended—since His

---

In the Quotations given above, it is maintained, that though the *Flesh* of CHRIST was sinful in itself, and "did carry up to His Mind every form of Seduction," yet that it neither *found* there any *Inclination* to Evil, or *left* there any *taint* of Pollution: neither did *He* commit Sin; because it is asserted that His WILL consented not to the Temptations presented to it by His sinful Flesh. In the *Orthodox and Catholic Doctrine,* (*Pref.* x.) Mr. *Irving* says, "we are steadily to bear in mind, that whenever he speaks of the *Flesh* of CHRIST he means the *whole Creature part,* (that is, His whole Human Nature,) except when the contrary is expressed:" and as in pa. 25, the *Flesh* of CHRIST is said to have "carried up to HIM" this every form of Seduction, &c. it is evident, from *Mr. Irving's* own words, that this "HIM" is the *Divine* Nature of CHRIST only; and that His Sinful *Human* Nature is thus made to tempt His *Divine, in which* it neither *found* nor *left* any Inclination to Evil; and hence he concludes, because His *Divine Nature* did not yield to the Temptation, that it is therefore to be said CHRIST did not sin, but *His* "*Will* abode in its Integrity, &c. thus making His *Divine* Nature only to constitute His *Person,* what time he else-where declares that CHRIST's *Person* is both *Human and Divine* (112,) two Natures in *one Person* united, (43,) and that "*No Act* is the Act of *either* Nature, but of the *Person,* including *both* Natures"—"CHRIST's *Person* being *in* His *Human* Nature as *much* as *in* His *Divine;*" and that "if His *Human* Nature *contradicted* His *Divine,* HE *is a* SINNER!" (70.)

It is also stated here, that CHRIST's Will *endured* all Temptations *just as* Mr. *Irving's* doth! But what saith the Scriptures? "He was in all points tempted like as we are, yet WITHOUT SIN!" *Heb.* iv. 15. Can Mr. *Irving* indeed presume to say this of *himself* when *he* is tempted? Is Mr. *Irving* "without sin," either *before,* or *under,* or *after* Temptation? Or is *his* tempted Will that of a *Divine Person?* If not, where is that great Analogy in the *endurance* of Temptation (for which Mr. *Irving* so earnestly contends) between CHRIST's Will and *his own?* The Will of CHRIST, which is made by Mr. *Irving* to be tempted, being that of the infinite and infallible CREATOR, *incapable* of *Passions,* but in *him* it is that of the poor, finite, sinful CREATURE, *full* of *Passions*—as above stated.

Having determined that CHRIST's *Divine* Nature *only* should constitute His *Person,* Mr. *Irving* tells us, (*Pref.* x.) that he can "assert the *Sinfulness* of the

whole Human Nature, both Soul and Body, is declared to have
been sinful, as disobedient "from first to last." And how
can it be said that "CHRIST's Flesh did carry up to His Mind
every form of Seduction; yet *left* it there no Sediment of
Evil, no Taint of Pollution, yet *found* it there no Response,
no Inclination, &c., if, as he elsewhere states, *every variety*

---

*whole Human Nature* which HE took, without *in the least* implicating HIM with
Sin." And in pa. 67, that "His Humanity, though in itself and of itself like
ours in all respects, was nevertheless not chargeable with any Sin." And all
this he asserts here, in open violation of his before- quoted Declarations on pa
86, that CHRIST's *whole Person* consisted of *both Natures*, Human and Divine"—
and in pa. 48, that he would not give the Truth expressed in these words of the
Catechism, "*Two distinct Natures*, and ONE PERSON for ever," for all the
Truths that by human language have ever been expressed." Again; that "*No
Act* is the Act of *either Nature*, but of the PERSON, including *both Natures*."(70.)
And yet he elsewhere asserts, that, "Every variety of Human Wickedness was
inherent in His Humanity!" That, "Through the faculties of the Human
*Soul*, He held communion with every impious, ungodly, and blasphemous
chamber of the fallen Intellect and feeling of Men." That, "His Flesh did,
carry up every form of Seduction to His Mind;" (or, to Him.) That "His
Flesh loved Temptation and ever conversed with the Tempter." (37.) And yet
after all this, he tells us, that this *Christ* of his was "without Sin"—because
forsooth, *Mr. Irving* is pleased to *say* so! and because *he* is pleased to make the
*Person* of CHRIST to consist of His *Divine* Nature *only* whenever it is found to
be convenient for his Error that it should be so! Thus it is in the following
quotations from pa. 10. "If then Christ was made under the Law, He must
have been made by His Human Nature *liable to*, yea, and *inclined* to all those
things which the Law interdicted. When I say inclined to, I speak of His *Human* Nature in *itself*, as contemplated *apart* from that *Divine* Nature which upheld it; from that PERSON of the SON OF GOD who *wrought* IN it, and BY it, the
Victory over all Sin." In the same way he separates between the two Natures
in CHRIST, by saying on pa. 31, "HE the SON OF GOD, was a *Holy One*, in
spite of *unholy Creation*:" (by which is meant *His Sinful Manhood*.) And so
again, on pa. 127. where he calls CHRIST's Sinless *Divine* Nature, "*I*," and
the *Human* Nature, (in which *he* says, "Sin inhered and tempted Him until the
Resurrection,") "His *Flesh*."

Keeping in mind that the *Divine* Nature *only* is made to be the *Person* of
CHRIST, we not only see why *Mr. Irving* makes the peculiar distinctions and
separations he does between the GODHEAD and the *Manhood*—calling the former His *Person*—"*He*"—"*Him*"—&c. and the latter, "The *Nature*," (*Pref.*
x.) "the Human *Substance*," (121.) "the whole *Creature-part*," (*Pref.* x.)
"the fallen *Creature*,"(121.) "the fallen *Man*,",(63.) "the fallen *Manhood*,"
(31.) "the rebellious *Creation* with which he clothed Himself," &c. (*Pref.* viii.)
but we discover why he attempts to establish a subtle distinction between *Sin*
in a *Nature* and *Sin* in a *Person*; (*Pref.* x.) and why he speaks of Sin being
"the condition of a *Person*," (87.) a "swaying of the *Person*," (44.) "the
act of the *Person*," (70.) "an act of the *Will*" only. (23, 73.) All these representations and distinctions being made by *Mr. Irving*, in order to shew how, in
his esteem at least, it can be said that *his Christ*, with a *fallen* Manhood, so *full*

of *Human Wickedness* was *inherent* in His Humanity, and that "He condescended, through the faculties of the *Human Soul* to *commune* with every impious, ungodly, and blasphemous Chamber, of the fallen Intellect and Feeling of Men!" It seems as if *Mr. Irving* considered *himself* at full liberty to assert any thing, however extravagant, in one page,

---

of *Sin* as he declares it to have been, was yet neither SINFUL nor yet a SINNER! Because His GODHEAD *only* being viewed as His *Person*, and Sin only as the *act* of the *Person*, His GODHEAD could not BE *sinful*, nor *commit* Sin—and therefore he maintains that *his false Christ* was *holy*, and not a *Sinner;* for "what was holy," he says, "was His *Person*," (*Pref.* x.) i. e. his *Divine* Nature, and this could not possibly commit a Sin in Thought, Word, or Deed.

Now, "Sin, in a *Nature*," we are told, by *Mr. Irving*, "is its *Disposition* to lead the *Person* away from GOD: Sin in a *Person*, is the *yielding* thereto;" (*Pref.* x.) and because the *Divine* Nature of CHRIST did not *yield* to the "Sinful Dispositions or Propensities" of His *Human* Nature, therefore *Mr. Irving* concludes this *his Christ!* was not a Sinner; although the *one Nature* "combined" against the *other*, and the one *tempted the other to the Commission of every Sin;* (17.) Declaring as he does, amongst other things, that CHRIST's "Sinful Flesh" was "Flesh of *that Kind and Property* which *betrayeth* and *tempteth* all other Persons unto Sin, and with *equal Force* wrought against the *Person* of the SON of GOD," (20.) All the weight of the Sinful Creation thus "concentrated (in CHRIST's Flesh) into one Hour and Power of Darkness; in His Agony and on His Cross, was permitted to *work amain* against the INCARNATE SON, (128.) when He did "so *endure* its *Vileness, withstand* its *Sinfulness, restrain* its *Propensities*, and present *it* free from any UNHOLY ACTION upon the Cross." (38.) And this is what he evidently means when he speaks of the PERSON of the SON of GOD, through the HOLY GHOST "*sustaining* His *Human Will* against the *Law* of the *Flesh*, (the *Sinful Propensities* of His *inherently Sinful Manhood*) in its largest and most comprehensive activity," (30.) or, "presenting his Creature-will sustained against all visible, sensible Oppositions, in perfect Harmony with the Will of GOD;" (31.) "Every variety of *Human Wickedness* being inherent in the Humanity," (17.) and inhering therein from the Incarnation to the Resurrection, (127.) the *Flesh* of CHRIST, ("His whole creature-part," *Pref.* x.) did carry up to HIM every form of Seduction!" (25.) or, in other words, more plain yet not more truly appalling, the Sinful Manhood of CHRIST became the very *Pander* of *Satan* in order to tempt the very GODHEAD of CHRIST! Such Manhood, or Flesh, be it remembered, *Mr. Irving* having described as "the *same* on which *Satan* has *triumphed* ever since the Fall," (40.) "*ever* LOVING *the* TEMPTATION and *ever* CONVERSING *with the* TEMPTER," (37.) "*Devil-minded*," (132). "*Devil-possessed*," (40.) and *out of which* the *Devil* was not cast until the morning of the Resurrection;" (67.) "All Sin," and "all *Devils*," amongst other things, having inhabited His Manhood until that period, when *Mr. Irving* informs us they were "all *strangled*" by the SON OF GOD! (8.) How then, in the face of his own before-quoted definition of Sin, that it is "any want of Conformity to, or Transgression of the Law of GOD"—and in the face of his own admissions, that CHRIST was a Person of *two* Natures—that His Person was in *both*—and His Acts those of neither Nature separately considered, but of the *Person* inhabiting both Natures—how, I say, can any one

(if it did but suit his own purpose,) and to advance something else, though in direct contradiction thereto on another:
and yet, that no one was to *presume* to call *His* judgment in
question under the penalty of his anathematizing them!

---

make such Statements as the foregoing, under the pretence of their being some
of " those high Points of Truth and Reason," or how can they be received by
others as the Discoveries of extraordinary Light, unless Darkness had possessed
the Minds of those who *made* such Statements, and gross Darkness fallen upon
their Minds who *received* them!        " If the Light that is in thee *be* Darkness,
HOW *great is* that Darkness!" *Matt.* vi. 23.

The GODHEAD of CHRIST being thus viewed as His *Person,* might also be
noticed as one way by which *Mr. Irving* attempts to justify his oft repeated
Declarations, that although CHRIST's Manhood was Inherently *Sinful* in itself,
yet that it was ever *upheld Holy,* or kept from committing outward *Acts* of
Sin " by GODHEAD *Power.*"  As this view, however, will fall in under the
Head of CHRIST's *Holiness,* I design noticing it in another place; observing
here, that the *Divine* Nature being thus viewed as the *Person* of CHRIST, affords
us the Key of Interpretation to many such expressions as the following : " HE
took the Prey out of the Hands of the Mighty.  HE gave *Satan* no Lodgment or
Residence; HE gave Sin no Quarters within His Being." (26.)  Here the GOD-
HEAD is the " HE," that took the Prey (that is, the Manhood) out of the hands
of the Mighty, (that is, *Satan;*) and the " Being," within which neither Sin nor
Satan had any Quarters given them, is the *Divine Nature* of CHRIST; since of the
Human it is said, " *Every variety of Human Wickedness* was inherent *therein.*"
In this view, also, we see how " *Satan* came and found nothing in HIM;"
this " HIM" being considered as the *Divine* Nature *only;* in which, of course,
no Sin ever was, or ever will be found.  Many similar Quotations might be
added under this Head, but the above must suffice.

Contradictions upon Contradictions here meet us again from *Mr. Irving's*
own Statements, take whatever view you will of the PERSON of *His Christ,* either
with or without His *Sinful Manhood,* either with or without his *inferior Godhead* or " Christhood."        1. View the *essential* GODHEAD only as the *Person,*
and you deny the Incarnation of the SON of GOD—His Atoning Sacrifice—the
Salvation of His Church—and all that pretended Similarity for which *Mr. Irving*
contends between CHRIST and his People under Temptation.        2. View the
*inferior* or limited *Godhead,* or *Christhood,* as the *Person,* either alone or in
union with the essential or absolute GODHEAD of the SON, and all the above
Contradictions and Objections again recur.        3. View the " *Sinful Manhood*
either in Union with the " absolute GODHEAD," or with the " limited" one,
or with both in Union, and the *Christ* thus constituted is made a Sinner, and
the Sentence of Blasphemy has gone forth from *Mr. Irving's* pen against the
Blasphemer! (pa. 2.)  Thus, having wandered from the good old way, *Mr.
Irving* has lost himself in the interminable Windings of his own Reasonings,
and entangled his Sentiment in the intricate Mazes of his own Error; from
which no Power that is merely human can ever extricate him, or set him free.
And great indeed will be the Mercy manifested to any of those, who, having
either preached, or cordially embraced, the *Sinfulness* of the Human Nature of
" the HOLY ONE of GOD," shall be brought to renounce it as a Pestilent
Heresy, subversive of every thing that has respect to the *glorious* PERSON of the

But the wise man has said, "He that is first in his own cause seemeth just, but his neighbour cometh and searcheth him."* If, however, this Will of Christ of which *Mr. Irving* speaks, "never consented to the Evil" but always

---

Lord Jesus Christ, and consequently destructive of every thing that relates to his *gracious* Salvation.

"*Nevertheless,* what saith the *Scripture ?*" "Behold, I lay in Sion, a *Chief Corner-Stone, Elect, Precious :* and he that *believeth* on Him shall not be confounded. Unto *you* therefore which *believe* He is *precious :* but unto them which be disobedient, the *Stone* which the *Builders* disallowed, the same is *made* the *Head* of the *Corner,* and a *Stone* of *Stumbling,* and a *Rock* of *Offence* even to *them* which *stumble* at *the Word,* being disobedient : whereunto also they were appointed." 1 *Peter* ii. 6, 7, 8.

* *Mr. Irving* seems to express, in very feeling terms, *his* "Charity and Love," towards those "Sectaries and Schismatics—the *Coles* and the *Haldanes,*" as he is pleased to call them ; and well he may ; for, like *Micaiah* of old, they "do not prophecy good concerning him, but evil." And therefore he seems to bestow on them a measure of the same love that the King of *Israel* conferred upon the Prophet of the Lord, of whom we read in 1 *Kings* xxii. 8.

"It is the fashion to accuse me of being abusive and personal," (*Mr. Irving* observes, in his *Orthodox Doctrine, Pref.* xi.) "It is not true of me either as a Man or a Writer. *I defy* them to produce out of *my* writings *one Word* of Uncharitableness towards the Person of any one." Let the following Gleanings be presented in answer to *Mr. Irving's* Challenge ; gathered as they have been from the very plentiful Harvest afforded by him in the very Tract in which he has dared the Proof; and *by them* let the Expressions of the Author of these Notes be tried, in his "carriage of *himself*" with "*unsparing destructiveness* towards erroneous Doctrines."

1. His *Opponents,* he calls his Enemies ; who, until they walk by *his* Rule of Love, shall flounder on in Error, and never come to see or love the Truth. (*Pref.* xii.) Railers, and Ignorant Persons, pa. 2. (in the *Morning Watch* they are termed "Railers and *Fools,*" 421.) Empty ones—Idle ones—13. Ignorant Alarmists—20. Pharisaical or Foolish Men—21. Under a strong Delusion from God—23. The ignorant Multitude, whom Blind Guides are deceiving unto their Destruction—23. Deceivers, and Anti-Christ—21. Blind Men—39. Debtor-and-Creditor Divines—46. Men who have gotten a Name—52. Deluders and deluded—51. Unlearned Clerks and evil-speaking Men—64. Gainsayers —63, 87. These Disputers of this World—68. Evangelicals, who do nauseate and repudiate the true Doctrine — 58. Those Hordes of Sectaries, (and unlearned Churchmen) who have risen up around us, and proclaim, in their several slanderous Publications, that it is a Heresy that Jesus Christ took sinful Flesh—21. The self-sufficient Leaders and Guides of the Religious World, compared with poor bewildered *Bourignon*—"that fond enthusiastic Woman"— that Mystic—an odious Name—who, with "all her unsober Fancies,"—with all her "heterodox Opinions,"—with all her impious, pernicious, blasphemous, and damnable Doctrine, was both a more honest Interpreter of Scripture, and a better Logician, Woman as she was, than they—66, 55. Hordes of Sectaries and Schismatics—86, 120. Revivers of old Heresies—87. Malicious Men ! Wicked Railers ! who will not learn Charity and Love—91. Adversaries of the

chose the Good, it could not have been a sin*ful* but a sin*less*
Will ; and, of course, not the Will of the "Apostate Creature," whose Nature, he says, CHRIST assumed, "with all its
inherent Propensities." Let us for a moment view it as the

---

Will of the *Divine* Nature, or of the GODHEAD of CHRIST; and then how contradictory does *Mr. Irving's* statement appear in reference to that *great similarity of Nature* which he contends for between CHRIST and Sinners, in order to His

---

Mixture of Human Nature and the HOLY GHOST—a Confusion of GODHEAD and Manhood—119. Their ruinous Schemes—120. A most strange Delusion, a strong Delusion—120. More like the Madness of the Maniac among the Schismatics—120. The Devil's Lie, which cannot be held, nor favoured, nor borne with, save at the greatest Risk and Peril to Immortal Souls—122. Which brings the Persons of the TRINITY into Confusion with one another, and with the Creature, and makes void Revelation in the Mass—122. A new Form of the Ancient Errors—128. Spurious Views of our LORD's Humanity—128. The Spurious and Heretical Tenets of those who hold CHRIST's Flesh or Human Nature to have been *Inherently Holy*—130. This Heretical Doctrine, from which a Thousand other most Fatal Practical Errors flow—140. The Radiating Point of Error—141. The present Fabric of Ignorance and Error, which Men have sanctified with most specious Names—142. Their Destructive and Seductive Errors—142. A Monstrous Thing, and never heard of in the Church until now—151. Their wretched Soul-destroying Error—153. A vile and abominable Fiction—154. A Doctrine that is Damnable; that to believe it is to believe a Lie, to die in the Faith of it is to die in the Faith of a Lie: and which like every Lie, (he believes) will work the Glory of the *Devil*, who was a Liar from the beginning, and not the Glory of JESUS CHRIST—141.

3. Their *Assertions, Mr. Irving* calls, Violent and Indiscriminate Attacks on the Truth—4. An Ignorance, not to say wicked Slander and abominable Calumny in those Hordes of Sectaries and Schismatics—86. Ignorance, however solemnly and doctorally it may be announced—52. A thing nonsensical, if *Christ's Humanity* were unfallen—88. The Wicked Surmises of Evil Tongues (that *he* leads to *Socinian* Views on the Subject of the Atonement.)—90. This wicked Charge—62. This abominable Insinuation, (that he leads to *Bourignonism*)—108. The Dogmatism of Ignorance—87. The Stock-jobbing Theology of the Religious World—95. Barbarous Ideas of God—98. This pure Ignorance and entire Emptiness of all Principles, which make so many fall into the Snare of the *Devil*—100. The one false View of a great Truth, with which the Evangelical part of the Church is poisoned—101. Branding the Truth with the name of Heresy—87. The Inventions of thoughtless Men, imposed upon the Church instead of the Truth of GOD—118. Argumentation without Argument—119. The present Fabric of Ignorance and Error, which Men have sanctified with the most specious Names—142.

"Now, what less can we say of these Words, but what the *General Assembly*" said of the Words of *Antoinette Bourignon!* " that they are fraught with great Errors." Where is *Mr. Irving's* boasting then, as to his *pre-eminent Orthodoxy*? Or where his loud Challenge, that he defies any one to produce out of his Writings *one Word* of Uncharitableness towards the Person of any one? It is excluded. By what means? The Assertions of his Adversaries? Nay; but by the Productions of his own pen; which have far surpassed all the utterances of " those Hordes of Sectaries and Schismatics," " those *Malicious Men!* those *Wicked Railers!*" as *Mr. Irving* is pleased to call his Opponents, as before mentioned, and concerning whom he also exclaims, "When will ye learn Charity and Love?"—91.

perfectly sympathizing with them under Temptation; for, in CHRIST, the Will tried is that of the *Infinite* CREATOR, *incapable* of *Passions;* but, in *Us,* it is that of the *Sinful Creature, full* of *Passions.\** And yet *Mr. Irving* says, that CHRIST's Will endured *all* Temptations *as his* doth; and that *He* was tempted in all points *like* as *Mr. Irving* is; when it is a poor fallible *Creature's* Will that is tempted in *Mr. Irving,* and (as his Statements would make it appear) the *infallible Creator's* Will which was tempted in CHRIST! Amazing disparity in the PERSONS, and Natures, and yet not the smallest possible difference in their susceptibility of Impressions, or endurance of Temptations!

Under this head, as well as under various others, the most unscriptural Statements, and palpable Contradictions, continually meet us from *Mr. Irving's* pen. In *one* page we read of the *Divine* Nature of CHRIST being *Self-existent* —in a *second, derived,* or *"taken* OF the FATHER"—in a *third,* " SELF *contracted"*—in a *fourth, "receiving* the HOLY GHOST"—and in a *fifth,* condescending OUT OF the *Godhead* INTO "this mass of Iniquity," and IN IT "toiling, sweating, and travailing, in exceeding great sorrow." In *one* page we find CHRIST described as having a sin*ful* Body and a sin*ful* Soul—in *another,* that HE was sin*less*—in a *third,* that He was *always* in the state of a regenerate Person—and in a *fourth,* we read of HIS Regeneration!—and in a *fifth,* that no change whatever had passed upon either His Body or Soul anterior to the Resurrection! In *one* page, that every variety of human "Wickedness was *inherent* in His Humanity"—which was "sinful Substance"—and in *another* that "*all* was holy, lovely, beautiful, and perfect, as the Will

---

* These *Three* Wills *Mr. Irving* has now reduced to *Two;* the *absolute* Will of the GODHEAD, and the *limited* Will of the *Manhood,* (*Orth. Doc.* pa. 54.) The GODHEAD, Infinitely *Holy*—the *Manhood,* inherently *Sinful;* and yet he maintains, that, *without* the smallest possible *Change,* the two Wills of these *opposite* Natures were *ever harmonious!* (54, 63.) How these TWO *Wills,* whether harmonious, or *inharmonious,* are to be distributed between the THREE *distinct* NATURES *Mr. Irving* has given to the *Christ* he has set up, in pa. 143, 145, would puzzle even the Inventor himself to explain. For, in the pages last mentioned, the *Person* of *his* Christ is made by *Mr. Irving* to consist, 1st. of His " Absolute GODHEAD;" 2ly. of a *Godhead not* absolute, (which *he* terms " *Christhood,"*) and 3ly. of a *Sinful Manhood!!!* Distinct Affections, and distinct Actions, being predicated of all *Three!* If *this* be *Mr. Irving's Orthodox* Doctrine, and the *Orthodox* Doctrine of his boasted " Mother Church," what shall we call *Heterodox!*                 *Isa.* viii. 20.

of GOD!" In *one* page, that CHRIST's Human Nature " differed not in any degree from our's in its alienation and guiltiness"—and in *another*, that in "His Mind there was no thought or meditation of Evil, Lust, Anger, Malice, or Hatred!" In *one* page, that His Soul and Body were " sinful to the last"—in *another*, that there was " a Work wrought therein by the HOLY GHOST"—and that they were both " holy, and presented to GOD without Spot." In *one* page, that through the faculties of the Human Soul He held Communion with all Wickedness in Men—in *another*, that in CHRIST's Mind there was " no Response, no Inclination to Evil, but Abhorrence and Detestation of the deepest, powerfullest kind." In *one* page, His Humanity is represented as the Strong-hold of Sin, and under its *inherent* Dominion—and in *another* it is declared, that " Sin had no Quarters within His Being." In *one* page, that CHRIST " DID *no* Sin"—and in another, that "His Flesh carried up every form of Temptation to His Mind," and that HE *held Communion* with every variety of Human Wickedness"— and was made under a Law which *Mr. Irving* says was only " made for a *sinful* Thing!" In *one* page, that CHRIST could not be chargeable with original Sin—in *another*, that His Body and Soul were both inherently Sinful—and His Flesh the *same* as *Mary's, David's,* and *Abraham's*—and *sinful Flesh of* their *sinful* flesh"—" accursed in the Loins of our first Father, *Adam*"—and that " CHRIST died because of the *common Property* of *Flesh to* die." That CHRIST's Body or Flesh " was corruptible, *proved* it to be fallen Flesh to the last; that it did not see Corruption, proved it to have been *sinless!*" " That his *Soul* descended into Hell (Hades), *proved* it to be a *fallen* Soul; that it came forth thence, *proved* it to be *holy!*"* **441.** But the time would fail me to enumerate

---

* Some of *Mr. Irving's* Friends have observed to the Author of this Letter, when he has pointed out to them the contradictory nature and destructive tendency of the preceding Statements, that " *Mr. Irving* never *meant* the erroneous things complained of, although they could not but allow that he had *stated* them as plainly as words could make them; witness the *Sinfulness* of CHRIST's Human Nature, which," say they, " *Mr. Irving* always asserts was altogether *holy!*" But if we are to judge of what *Mr. Irving means* by what he *says*, and his own Declarations committed to writing and published to the World under the title of " Catholic and Orthodox Doctrine," and with the express design of curing the " unsound Faith of many," and of settling the " insecure and unsteady Faith of almost all in the *true* Humanity of CHRIST," are of any Authority in

*all* the unscriptural Expressions, false Assumptions and
Assertions, unjust Conclusions, and manifest Contradictions,

---

this case, it is evident that either *Mr. Irving* " knows not what he says nor
whereof he affirms," or that his *sayings* contradict what he *means!* Whatever
mental Reservation *Mr. Irving* may have in making some of the Statements he
has done, I know not; but if Words in the *English* language have any defined
meaning, and *Mr. Irving's* words, in common with other Persons', are to be
considered " the Reports of the Mind," his " Tractate" on " The Orthodox and
Catholic Doctrine of our LORD's Human Nature" will be sufficient Witness in
proof of his Self-contradiction, without its being in any degree " *tortured* to
mean" what the terms used do not justly convey to the enlightened Mind.

Some other Persons, who are not considered *Mr. Irving's* Friends in particular, from having read his Letter in " *The Times*" of Thursday, the 14th of
*October* last, (wherein he repels the charge made against him and a *Mr. Scott*,
of holding " that our LORD's *Human* Nature was *Sinful*," by avowing that, on
the contrary, they maintain with all *Orthodox* Men that it was " *without Sin*,")
have naturally concluded, and upon such Authority have naturally reported,
that *Mr. Irving* had publicly disclaimed holding that truly erroneous and exceedingly dangerous Doctrine; and nothing short of *Mr. Irving's* numerous
and palpable Contradictions of himself in the Tract before mentioned, could
induce them to think that a professed Minister of CHRIST, of such elevated rank
too as " THE *Minister of* THE NATIONAL SCOTCH *Church in* LONDON," could in
his heart believe, that the Human Nature of JESUS was FULL of *Sin* what time
his own words positively declared that it was " WITHOUT *Sin*." *Mr. Irving's*
very words, as copied from *The Times*, are these :

" The third (charge) is, that our LORD's Human Nature was *Sinful*,
" whereas WE maintain, with *all Orthodox Men*, that it was " WITHOUT SIN," by
" the anointing of the HOLY GHOST."

But —*Mr. Irving* HAS NOT renounced the Error, nor relinquished one *Iota*
of the Statement previously made by him in his " Orthodox and Catholic Doctrine of our LORD's Human Nature," that " *every variety* of *human* PASSION,
*every variety* of *human* AFFECTION, *every variety* of *human* ERROR, *every variety*
of *human* WICKEDNESS, which hath ever been realized, was inherent in the Humanity of the SON of GOD," (p. 17.) But, on the contrary, he assures us again
and again, in the same publication, that " In its natural Propensities, therefore, he indubitably holds, and to the Death will maintain, and for the Faith of
it shall have to praise GOD through Eternity, that CHRIST's *Human Nature*, His
*undivided Manhood*, was *in all respects* as *ours*"—that is, just as *sinful* as ours,
(pa. 110.) " That to yield a *jot* of this is to yield *all:* that he will not yield a *jot*
of it. He will suffer the loss of all things, sooner, and *Death itself*, than
suffer this Doctrine to be shaken so long as he can help it." (pa. 111.) That " he
will maintain it unto Death," (pa. 63.) That, " for his own part he has taken
his ground, and will contend there unto the Death; and so the Enemy knows
where to find him;" (pa. 124.) So that, if the Devil *himself* with all his Legions
dared to stand up and impugn *these eternal Truths*, (the " evil Propensities"
of the fallen Manhood of CHRIST being enumerated as a very conspicuous
one among them) he " would uphold them against him for ever !" (pa. 64.)
And then, like some faithful Soldier, " enduring hardness in a better cause,"
" attempered and annealed for the proof" (amidst what *Mr. Irving* calls the
sensative shrinkings and misgivings of ignorant Alarmists"—that is, the apprehension of unseared Consciences, pa. 20) as a mighty Captain in his Master's

that are contained in *Mr. Irving's* production on "the *true* Humanity of CHRIST"—in which His anathematizing Spirit

---

service, he comes forth from that high " Region" or Sphere " of Thought and Reasoning," (in which, he says, *we* " poor ignorant ones" are not accustomed to think, (131) with this Word of command to " his Brethren who are stirred up to do battle over men for the bulwarks of ZION," (or, in other words, to oppose those who maintain the *inherent* HOLINESS of the *Humanity* of JESUS,)

" *Spare* the men ; but, Oh ! *spare not* THE ERROR, ATTACK IT, EXPOSE " IT, ROOT IT OUT, DESTROY IT ; and let the *last breath* be a TESTIMONY " AGAINST IT !" (142.)

*Mr. Irving*, therefore, I repeat, by his public avowal in " *The Times*," has NOT renounced, and in the above Quotations from his " *Orthodox Doctrine*," he assures us that he *never will renounce* even " *one jot*" of all that he has asserted concerning the *inherent Sinfulness* and *innate Wickedness* he has so awfully attributed to the Human Nature of the LORD JESUS CHRIST ! Why then should *Mr. Irving* have couched his real sentiments in such words as those above quoted, if he really had no intention to deceive the ignorant and unwary, who knew not that, in the very moment in which he penned that repelling declaration " Whereas, (that is, " on the contrary,") WE maintain, with *all Orthodox men*, that it was " *without sin*," in that very moment *Mr. Irving* had a mental Reservation *how* he could nevertheless *hold*, and boldly *assert* " the SINFULNESS of the WHOLE, the COMPLETE, the PERFECT *Human Nature* which JESUS took, without in the least implicating HIM with *Sin !*" (*Pref.* x.)

And who could have *supposed*, after having read 153 pages and the Preface of *Mr. Irving's* " Tractate," written for the express purpose of *asserting* and *vindicating* the *inherent* SINFULNESS of the Human Nature of the SON OF GOD, from its Conception in the Virgin until its Resurrection from the Tomb—who could have *imagined*, after having noticed the dreadful *Anathemas* therein dealt out against all those who maintain the *inherent* HOLINESS of " that HOLY THING" which was born of the Virgin—who could even have *dreamt*, after having noticed the " *unsparing destructiveness*" so openly avowed throughout his whole work against the *inherent* HOLINESS of the *Humanity* of JESUS, and after having weighed the exterminating edict put forth, as above, to " *attack* it, *expose* it, *root it out*, and to *destroy* it," that MR. IRVING HIMSELF should, on the 154th and last page of his work, have closed his long, and loud, and deep LAMENT over the " unsound Faith of many," over the " insecure and unsteady Faith of almost *all*, in the *true* Humanity of CHRIST, in these remarkable words :

" Ah ! it is a *fearful* Siege which is at present carrying on against the *very Citadel* of GOD'S OWN HOLY BEING, and man's free Inheritance in His Grace ; and WE, who should have been as one man to *defend* GOD'S HOLY BEING, and our own goodly Inheritance in His Grace, *are* like the sons of *Ephraim* DRUNKEN, but *not* with *wine* or *strong drink*—DRUNKEN WITH DELUSION AND THE CUP OF ERROR !"

*Who* is it then, I ask, that has commenced, and at the present carries on this " Siege," this " *fearful* Siege" against the " *very* CITADEL of GOD's own *Holy Being*"—but *that Individual* who so fearlessly asserts, that " *every variety* of *Human Wickedness* was *inherent* in the *Manhood* of the SON OF GOD ?"

*Who* is it, I enquire, that wrests the Holy Scriptures (even to his own destruction, if Grace prevent not) in order to *attack* the *inherent* HOLINESS of the SON of MAN—but MR. IRVING ?

hands over to Perdition the most venerable and valuable Servants of the LORD who have ever adorned the Church of GOD, because they follow not with him—because they have not believed His perilous alteration of Holy Scripture, that "JESUS

---

*Who* is it that, "through Philosophy and vain Deceit," has first attempted to corrupt, and then to destroy, but every Doctrine of the pure Word of GOD, by setting forth the *Sinfulness* of the Human Nature of the LORD JESUS—but MR. IRVING?

*Who* is it that pretends to shew that the Church of CHRIST, in all its ancient *Creeds*, or Symbols of the Christian Faith, has ever maintained the *Sinfulness*, the *inherent Sinfulness* of one part of the great OBJECT of her FAITH and HOPE —but MR. IRVING?

*Who* is it that has marshalled his perverted Testimonies of the *ancient Fathers* and *modern Reformers* of the Christian Church, against the *inherent Holiness* of the MAN CHRIST JESUS, the Church's *Foundation* and the Church's *Head*—but MR. IRVING?

*Who* is it that proclaims it to be "the *Devil's Lie*," and "*a damnable Heresy*," to hold that "CHRIST's Human Nature was *inherently* HOLY"—and who *anathematizes* all those who do—but MR. IRVING?

*Who* is it that lays down the INHERENT SINFULNESS of the Human Nature of the LORD JESUS, as the "One only FOUNDATION of the *Orthodox Faith*"— (2, 54) of the Christian's *Hope* and *Consolation*—and the Doctrine of the *inherent* HOLINESS as having "perilous Issues"—"fatal Consequences"— and "subverting all Foundations, to which it tends"—Who, but MR. IRVING?

*Who* is it that "believes it to be MOST *Orthodox*, and of the *Substance* and *Essence* of the Orthodox Faith, to hold that CHRIST could say *until* His *Resurrection*, NOT I, BUT SIN THAT TEMPTETH ME IN MY FLESH—that the *only* difference between His Body of Humiliation and His Body of Resurrection *is* in *this very thing*, that SIN INHERED in the *Human Nature*, making it *mortal* and *corruptible, till that very time that He rose from the dead:*" and that "IF THIS PRINCIPLE MUST GO TO THE WALL, I SHALL GO TO THE WALL ALONG WITH IT!"—Who *believes* and *asserts such Things*, but—MR. IRVING?

And, in one word—*Who* is it but MR. IRVING HIMSELF, that, "drunken with Delusion and the cup of Error," marshals the Host which he himself has taught "to stand the fire of the Christian Battle," as he terms it, (or, in other words, *hardened in Error*,) and with his "unsober Fancy" actuating his "unbridled Spirit," leads on the forlorn Hope to that truly "*fearful Siege*" he yet so deeply laments and so loudly deprecates—a "Siege" against the "very CITADEL of GOD's OWN HOLY BEING,"—the *Inherent* SINLESSNESS of GOD's HOLY CHILD JESUS!

But, blessed be GOD! no Attempt of *Mr. Irving's* can ever *undermine* this CITADEL *Divine!*—no Assault of his, from *any*, or from *all* those "Regions" of which he speaks, whether from *above*, or from *beneath*, can ever take it by *Storm*, or touch the Holy *City* that it guards! For "Thus saith the LORD GOD," "Behold I lay in *Zion* for a Foundation, a *Stone*, a *tried* Stone, a *Precious Corner-Stone*, a *Sure Foundation!*" (*Isa.* xxviii. 16.) "And on this ROCK will I build My Church, and the Gates of Hell shall not prevail against it." (*Matt.* xvi. 18.) So that in the face of all his Foes, *internal*, *external*, and *infernal*, the true Believer in the *Complex* PERSON and *Inherent* SINLESSNESS of GOD's HOLY

CHRIST came in *Sinful* Flesh!" and in which he so completely " condemns himself in the very thing that he allows."

As there can be no *justifying Righteousness* for a Sinner, in the sight of GOD, if *Mr. Irving's* Hypothesis be true,

---

CHILD JESUS, may still sing of his JEHOVAH-SHAMMAH,—"The LORD is there," —in the expressive language of our Christian Poet, COWPER:

> " Let *Earth* repent, and *Hell* despair,
> *This City* has a *sure* Defence;
> Her Name is call'd " THE LORD IS THERE,"
> And *Who* has Pow'r to drive HIM *thence?*"

" By what manner of misconception then"—to use *Mr. Irving's* own words—doth he here " put Darkness for Light, and Light for Darkness; Bitter for Sweet, and Sweet for Bitter?" " By what blindness of Error" doth he here " stretch out his hand against GOD, and strengthen himself against the ALMIGHTY? running upon Him, even upon His Neck, upon the thick Bosses of His Bucklers," in that " *fearful Siege* which is at present carried on against the very *Citadel* of GOD's *own* HOLY BEING," NOT indeed by *Mr. Irving's* Adversaries, as he would have it believed, but even by MR. IRVING HIMSELF! " Oh, it is a most STRANGE DELUSION, it is a STRONG DELUSION!" and into which surely he had never fallen had not " a deceived Heart turned him aside, that he cannot deliver his Soul, nor say is there not a Lie in my right hand!"

But *Mr. Irving's* Apologists have told us that " he does not *mean* what he *says!*" And so it must appear to every reader of his Letter in " *The Times*," when it is known that therein he has not *said* what he *means*, (which is, that he *does* believe our LORD's Human Nature was *sinful—inherently sinful*, and so remained until the Morning of the Resurrection—(pa. 127.) but that *Mr. Irving* has invented a way by which *his Christ* could be considered inherently *sin-FUL* and yet perfectly *sin-LESS*, in Himself and of Himself considered at one and the same time; and to know *how* that could be, he assures us is the " Alpha and Omega, the Beginning and the Ending of, *Orthodox Theology!*" (18.) " *I say* He took *sinFUL* Flesh and yet was *sinLESS*; and, moreover, *I say* that He died, and yet was sinless. If any man say that this is a matter of mere Words, *I tell him* that he hath yet to learn the Alphabet of his Theology," (86.) " And, moreover, I believe, that the only difference between His Body of Humiliation, and His Body of Resurrection, is in this very thing, that *Sin inhered* in the Human Nature, making it mortal and corruptible, until that very time that He rose from the dead."

And thus, upon the truly sandy Foundation of the " I SAY," and the " I SAY," of one whose Friends informs us that he does not *mean what* he *says*; and whose public avowal as quoted from " *The Times*" shews us that he does *not say* what he *means*, are we " poor ignorant ones" called upon to believe his awful Errors as the very Essence of the *Orthodox Faith*, under the apprehension of his Anathemas for not believing—not what is *revealed in* Holy Scripture, but his perilous *Addition to and Alteration of* Holy Scripture—namely, that our LORD JESUS CHRIST came in *Sinful* Flesh! and that Sin actually *inhered in* and tempted Him through the means of His dead Flesh, *after* He had *suffered* on the *Cross* and *before* He rose from the Grave!

Herein, those dreadful " Heretics" *Mr. Irving* reprobates, and all those " Hordes of Sectaries and Schismatics" he charges with " Ignorance, not to

(since it is not the *essential* Rectitude of the *Divine* Nature of CHRIST which is imputed, or placed to the account of His Church, but the Righteousness He *wrought out* as GOD-MAN, in going "to the end of the Law" under which He was made, as her Surety and her Head,\*) so neither can there be

---

say wicked Slander and abominable Calumny," (because they tell the World *the Truth*, in saying that *his* Doctrine makes CHRIST *a Sinner*—which, even on his own shewing it certainly does—) would much rather turn away from the Heterodox assertions of "THE Minister of THE National *Scotch* Church in London, and join in the Petitions of the Orthodox Clergy of "the Church of *England*, as by Law established," when they say,

"From *all false Doctrine, Heresy*, and *Schism; from hardness* of "*Heart*, ("*from all blindness of Heart*" too,) and from Contempt of Thy "Word and Commandment, (*Prov.* xxx. 6. *Rev.* xxii. 18.)

"GOOD LORD *deliver us!*"

\* Spoiled, "through Philosophy and vain deceit, after the Tradition of Men, and not after CHRIST," *Mr. Irving spoils* but every Doctrine he pretends to explain. That important one of the *Headship* of JESUS is of this number:— of which, in pa. 31, he says, "*After* His ASCENSION He *became* the HEAD of all *Believers*, the HEAD of all the *Elect*, the SAVIOUR of the *saved!*" What then became of all the *Old* Testament Saints, and all such as died *before* the *Ascension* of CHRIST under the *New*, if the above Theory be correct?—since every one of them must have lived and died *without* a *Saviour;* and *without* a *Head;* and, consequently, must have perished in their Sins! And how are *we* better off than *they*, if JESUS only became a Head *not* in *this* Life, but *after* His *Ascension?* Or how could He have been any *real Saviour*, even at *any period*, with such an *inherently Sinful Nature* as *Mr. Irving* uniformly ascribes to Him? *Mr. Irving* may indeed have invented this *post mortem* Headship, "as a misrepresentation to support his Theory," his Fundamental Article of Faith, "that *Sin inhered* in the Human Nature of CHRIST, making it mortal and corruptible, till that very time that He rose from the dead;" but it will assuredly turn out to be one of his own "unsober Fancies" which, to use his own words, "subverts all Foundations"—"makes His Manhood a Fiction, the Gospels an imaginary Tale, and Faith a foolish Fancy."

*Adam*, we know, was a Type of *Christ*. (Rom. v. 14.) And very strikingly is He so revealed in the Chapter just referred to; where *Adam* and CHRIST are spoken of as if they had been the only two Personages of any note, they being there exhibited as the two public Heads or Representatives of their respective Seeds; and the channels of communicating to them either Sin and Death, or Righteousness and Life. "*Adam*, before his fall," *Mr. Irving* says, was not only "*a Type*," but "the *only perfect* Type of CHRIST." (pa. 61.) And yet, in his wonted way of contradiction, he sometimes makes the greatest *dissimilarity* between them in some of the most essential points wherein they ought to have agreed; while in other Instances, of no small moment, he attributes to the *earthly Adam* the pre-eminence that exclusively belongs to the *heavenly* one.

1st. Observe that great DIS-*similarity* exhibited to us in the following words, (in pa. 9) that "*Adam* was NOT *under* the *Law*." While in the page preceding he had told us that CHRIST *was* "made under the Law." "To say, (he observes, pa. 9) that *Adam was* under the Law"—is only "to serve a

any *Holiness* for a Sinner, before GOD ; since CHRIST is not of GOD made unto His Church Sanctification, through the imputation of the *essential Holiness* of His *Divine* Nature, any more than He is made unto her *Righteousness* through the imputation of the *essential Rectitude* of His *Divine* Na-

---

System," and, " which may not be permitted :"—Whereas, in order to serve his *own System*, he not only makes the foregoing assertions, but the subsequent ones also ; namely, that " the Law *presupposeth* a *Sinful Condition*, and doth address itself thereto"—and therefore that " the *whole Ten Commands* were *inapplicable* to *Adam* (in innocence) he being made *perfect* and *good*, and *to no Theft inclined*." But " CHRIST *was* made under the Law"—the *whole* of which was *applicable* to HIM, because *His Human Nature*, it is asserted, was " *sinful* and *corrupt*," and " INCLINED TO EVERY EVIL that the *Law* interdicted !" (10.) " And the Law, (it is said by *Mr. Irving*) is not made for a *righteous Thing*, but for a *sinful Thing*." (22.) " Then, (he says, pa. 10,) " to be made under the Law MUST MEAN to be *put into* the *Condition* of a *fallen Creature !*" " If then, (it is added, pa. 10,) CHRIST *was* made under the Law, HE *must* have been made by His Human Nature *liable* to, yea, and *inclined* to, *all those things which the Law interdicted !*" (10.) " Now, if any one still allege that He might be under the Law, (it is continued in the same page 10,) and yet not come in *fallen* Human Nature, or in *Flesh* of SIN, but in Flesh of *Adam* UN-*fallen*, then I must just say to that Person, that either he denies that CHRIST was generated under Law, or he holds that *Adam unfallen* was under Law ; of which two Errors I know not whether be the greater." " It may not be permitted therefore (he concludes on pa. 9,) for any Person, in order to serve a System, to say, that *Adam was under the Law*, or even that *Abraham* was under the Law. If this liberty be allowed, *then I* can give *no Interpretation whatever* of the Expression " CHRIST made under the Law."       And so, in fact, because the *Truth* stands in the way of *Mr. Irving's erroneous Interpretation*, it must not be spoken ! But—" *Great is the* TRUTH *and it* WILL *prevail*."

In the preceding Quotations, I think we have the following amongst other " seductive and destructive Errors" and contradictory Statements presented to our view, namely, That the *first Adam* being HOLY, was *not* under *Law*—but that the *second*, being SINFUL, *was* under Law. Now, not to notice here, particularly, either the great dissimilarity thus made between the *first Adam*, in his created *Holiness*, and the *second*, in his supposed *Sinfulness*— or, the pre-eminence given to the *earthly Adam*, which of divine right exclusively belongs to the *heavenly One*—I would ask, How could *Sin* have entered into the World by *One* Man, and *Death* by *Sin*, and so *Death* have passed upon *all men*, as the consequence of *Sin*, if indeed the *first Adam* had *not* been under Law ? " Sin," *Mr. Irving* himself tells us, from the Creed of the Church of *Scotland*, " is any want of Conformity to, or Transgression of, the Law of GOD." (38.)    " And the Scriptures declare that where no Law is, there is *no Transgression*."—(Rom. iv. 15.) for, " by the Law is the knowledge of Sin." (Rom. iii. 20.) If therefore, the *first Adam* had *not* been under *Law*, how could he have been a *Sinner ?* It is evident that he *sinned*—and that he *suffered*—and that he *died* :—and these are so many *Consequences* of his having been under the Law, however *Mr. Irving*, " in order to serve a System," may think proper to *permit himself* to deny it. It is clearly revealed too, even in that very " Word of GOD" before which " *Mr. Irving* says " he is accus-

ture—but His People, as viewed perfectly *holy*, are so beheld in the *perfect Holiness* of the *created* Nature of the Complex Person of the GOD-MAN; just as they are viewed

---

tomed to tremble"—that *Adam*, having transgressed, had the *Curse* of the Law pronounced upon him for his Transgression, even by GOD himself—whereas, if *Adam* had *not* been under the Law, it is not only evident there had been *no Transgression* committed by him, but that the *Justice* of GOD had been impeached in pronouncing a *Curse* where neither the *Law* nor any *Sin* in any way existed! But—" shall not the Judge of all the Earth do right ?"

The Doctrine of *Original Sin* would thus be " distinctly or flatly denied, avoided, and destroyed," if it could be said with Truth (as *Mr. Irving* pretends it may,) that " *Adam* was *not* under the Law"—and that it is a " great Error to say that he *was* under it"—for, in *such* case, *Adam* himself must have been " *without* Sin," the Scriptures having assured us that where no Law is there is no Transgression !" and *Mr. Irving's* Charge against *us* of " destroying the *reality* of the *Fall*," (pa. 110,) recoils with a Vengeance upon the notions of *him* who made it ! By what right then, (to use his own expression) does *Mr. Irving* speak of "*Adam's* SIN"—(74,) of *Adam's* GUILT, (86,) of " his *guilty Soul* and *Sinful Flesh*"—(6,) of " the *Sin* and *Misery* into which *Adam* was brought by the FALL;"—(82,) Or, by what right does he ever *mention* even the term *Original Sin*"—or tell us " this is the *meaning* of it—that as *Adam* was, so are all his Posterity in the Sight of GOD, come they when they may upon the face of the visible World"—(133.) Since *Mr. Irving* himself has prevented the possibility of its occurrence, he having placed *his Adam* in that condition in which he could not have *committed* Sin, being, as he declares, " *not under Law !*" Who is it then that is found imposing his *own Inventions* upon the Church, instead of the *Truth* of GOD—*Mr. Irving*, or his Opponents? whom he denominates " Thoughtless Men"—" Empty ones"—" Idle ones"—" Ignorant Alarmists"—" Railers and Fools, &c. &c." ? (See the note, on pa. 53.)

I would also observe here, that as the *second Adam* really *was* made " under the Law," and (according to *Mr. Irving's* account,) the *first* was *not*, there is not only this great dissimilarity between the " most perfect Type" (as he *calls Adam*) and the Antitype, but these contradictory things immediately assail us—that the *second Adam* must have " magnified and made honourable" a Law which could not have been *transgressed* in any thing by the *first*—that the *first*, not having *sinned*, needed not to be *saved*, any more than the Elect Angels who kept their first Estate—that both the Righteousness and Bloodshedding of the SECOND ADAM were useless things as to the *first*—and that *Original Sin* could not have been justly chargeable on any of *Adam's Seed*, since he himself, not being " under Law," could not have been guilty of any Transgression ! Certain manifest impossibilities also, would result from *Mr. Irving's* false premises :—the first, or *sinful* Adam, if *not* " under Law, is placed in a condition in which *he* could not have become a *Sinner*—while the *second*, or *holy Adam*, in possessing an inherently *sinful* Nature, is brought into a state in which *He* could not have become a *Saviour !* In pa. 151, it is said that CHRIST'S Human Nature was held of *Sinful Adam*"—and that the part that He took was subject to the *same Laws* as the Lump of which He took it." And yet, in pa. 9, GOD's *holy Adam* was not under any *one* of the Ten Commands in the Law—while *Mr. Irving's sinful Christ* was made under them *all*, and " *inclined* to all those things which the Law interdicted." (10.) Here then we

perfectly *righteous* in the perfect *Obedience* of the GOD-
MAN ;—but if CHRIST's Human Nature were, (as *Mr. Irving*
declares it to have been) "sinful"—no Holiness could have

---

have, an inherently *holy Adam sinning*, where there was no Law to trans-
gress; and an *inherently sinful Adam* working out a *Righteousness* in a nature
that possessed " every variety of Human *Wickedness !*"

2ʸ. The other great dissimilarity I would more particularly notice here, as
made by *Mr. Irving* between the *second Adam* and the *first*, is, in their *Headships*,
of Representations of their respective Seeds :—the *former*, being viewed as a
head in *this* Life ; but the *latter*, only in the Life *to come !* His words are
these : " After his Ascension He (CHRIST) became the HEAD of all *Believers*,
the HEAD of all the ELECT, the SAVIOUR of the *saved*"—(pa. 31 ;) and in pa.
139, he says, " It is a mere misinterpretation to support a Theory, to call Him
the *Second Adam* till his Ascension into Glory : but it is very convenient for
sustaining the *erroneous Doctrines* of His Life and Death being only for a *part ;*
for *if* He was the *second Adam* in the Flesh, *then His Action* must respect *only*
the *Children* of the *second Adam*, that is, the *Elect exclusively :*" and thus, in
the second quotation, *Mr. Irving* shews us how he secretly fights against that
very Doctrine of *Election* which he professes to hold with in the *first ;* asserting as he does on pa. 139, that " to call Him the *second Adam* till his *Ascension*
was convenient for sustaining the *erroneous Doctrines* of His Life and Death
being only for a *part*"—" the *Elect exclusively ;*" while in pa. 31, he positively affirms that " *After* His *Ascension* HE *became* the HEAD of *all* THE
ELECT !"

In addition to the remarks already made under the first dissimilarity, that
" *Adam* was not under the Law," which in many respects are as applicable to
this second one, that *Christ* was not " the *Head* of all the Elect until *after* His
*Ascension*," I observe, that if the LORD's CHRIST were not the " *Head of His
Body* the *Church*" anterior to His Ascension, He must have been, up to that
very period, a *private Person only*, and *not* a *public Head* or Representative, all
the time He tabernacled amongst us. All that He did, and all that He suffered,
He must, consequently, have done and have suffered AS a *private Person*, IN a
*private Capacity only ;* yea, for *Himself alone*—in open violation of all those
Scriptures that declare Him to have been " *wounded* for *our* Transgressions—
" *bruised* for *our* Iniquities—and to be " cut off—but *not* for *Himself*—for though
" He had done no violence, neither was any deceit found in His mouth, yet it
pleased the LORD to bruise *Him*"—the Head being smitten, that all the Members might go free—He, as the Head, restoring that which His Members only
had taken away. But if the Headship of CHRIST be denied, or destroyed, so
must His Body, the Church, also—for the Head and Members must live together, or together die.

That " more sure word of Prophecy, unto which we do well to take heed,
as unto a light that shineth in a dark place," testifies to us of GOD's CHRIST,
" who verily was fore-ordained CHRIST before the foundation of the World"—
(1 *Pet.* i. 20,) of Him, who was " set up from everlasting"—(*Prov.* viii. 23.)
" Whose goings forth had been from of old"—(*Mich.* v. 2,) as " JEHOVAH's
Servant whom He upheld, His Elect, in whom His soul delighted." (*Isa.*
xlii. l.) The same unerring Testimony exhibits to our view the Elect *Members* as *loved*, and *chosen*, and *blest*," with all spiritual Blessings in heavenly
places in CHRIST JESUS, (their Elect Head) before the World began"—(*Eph.* i. 3.

been imputed to them through CHRIST—for, in such case,
even He Himself had no Holiness in His *Human* Nature,

---

*John* xvii. 23, 24. As "full of Grace and Truth—and of whose fulness had
all (Believers) received, and Grace for Grace"—(*John* i. 14, 15.) JESUS, as the
Head, being not only the receptacle of all spiritual Blessings, but the only Way
of their being communicated to His People. But if *Mr. Irving's* statement be
true, that it was only "after His Ascension that CHRIST became the Head of
all Believers," not only are all those Scriptures set at naught, wherein He is
set forth as *being* ALL TO His People—*having* ALL FOR His People—and *doing*
All on their Account, but the very Foundation of the Church is at once sub-
verted, and the Hope of the Righteous for ever destroyed! Such a statement
as *Mr. Irving's* concerning the *Headship* of the LORD JESUS CHRIST, may probably be hailed by those who are Enemies to His *Person;* but by all such true
Believers in Him as *know* that JESUS is JEHOVAH, by the Revelation of the
HOLY GHOST, (1 *Cor.* xii. 3.) it must ever be lamented, and will ever be deplored,
in the exact proportion as the effects of *Mr. Irving's* Error is perceived, and
the Truth of GOD is enjoyed. For, if JESUS of *Nazareth* were not our Head
when He was upon Earth, all His Obedience, Sufferings, and Death, (as has
been already observed) were those of a *Private* Individual only—were for *Himself alone*—as a mere *Man*—and not as "GOD-MAN Mediator, for all those in
whose room and stead He came to obey, to suffer, bleed, and die," as an Offering and a *Sacrifice* to GOD "of a sweet-smelling savour;" and not as the mere
Exemplar, or Pattern of enduring suffering, to any man, or to any set of men,
how diversified soever may be their grades, or shades, in *Socinianism*.

However *Mr. Irving* may sometimes speak of *his Christ* as the "*publicus
Homo*," (that is, the public Man) it should ever be remembered, that his *calling*
Him such, no more *makes Him* a public Head, than his *calling* His Human
Nature "fallen Manhood" really *makes* it, as proves it to have been, "sinful
Flesh and Blood." And although he says in pa. 112, that "it is a Truth
acknowledged in all Churches, as devoutly rested in by all Believers, that
CHRIST stands in the *Room* of sinful men," it is evident that this postponement
of CHRIST's Headship until *after this Life*, entirely removes the *Substitute* or
Public Head, during the most eventful and indispensably needful period of His
existence; just as the assertion that He assumed "fallen Manhood" into
union with His GODHEAD, would effectually destroy the possibility of any
acceptable obedience to GOD, and annihilate for ever all atoning efficacy in His
Blood. This delusive notion of a mere *post mortem* Headship of CHRIST, would
be of no more real service to the Church than would be the visit of the most
renowned earthly Physician to the House of a Patient after such a Patient had
departed into the World of Spirits. *Life—this* Life was the important period
for the services of the Physician of the Body; and Life, *this* Life was the
eventful period in which the great Physician of the Soul stood in the room and
stead of His People, and as their Head or Representative, Substitute and Surety,
went "to the end of the Law for Righteousness to every one that believeth."

Various other statements, both as unscriptural and as contradictory as the
foregoing, are made by *Mr. Irving* respecting the *Headship* of CHRIST in other
places; wherein he sets forth His Human Nature as being not only GEN-*erated*,
but RE-*generated* also by the HOLY GHOST at one and the same instant of Time,
(137) and yet, that the Issue *so gen*-erated and so *re*-generated also, was, nevertheless "SINFUL SUBSTANCE"—although the Holy Ghost declares it was "*That*

and the Holiness of the *Divine* not being imputable, could not have been imputed, and actually was not, and never will be!*

---

Holy Thing!" In one page, (124) *Mr. Irving* calls *his Christ* " the *first regenerate Man*"—" the *perfect* Man of Regeneration"—(*Pref.* viii.)—in another, (pa. 113,) the *Head* of the Regeneration"—in a third (pa. 110,) " the *great Head* of the regenerate race"—" entirely and wholly regenerated of the HOLY GHOST"—(78)—the *first*, the *complete regenerated Man* unto the end of being, (136)—and yet, in pa. 101, he asserts, that at the day of *Pentecost* was " the *first Act of Regeneration !!!*

. And what shall I say more concerning this false view of the *Headship* of CHRIST, than what *Mr. Irving* himself says of what *he* opposes in pa. 110; that it is " a Notion which destroys *Redemption*, which destroys the *reality* of the *Fall*, which destroys GOD's *Fellowship* with *us*, and in truth destroys *every thing worth the preserving.*" " It is this pure ignorance and entire emptiness of all Principles which make so many fall into the snare of the Devil: from which, O God! bless this endeavour to set them free."—*Ortho. Doc. pa.* 100.

* " The wild Hypothesis and most fearful Error," which *Mr. Irving* substitutes for the true Holiness of " The LORD's CHRIST," as revealed in the Holy Scriptures of Truth, occupies so conspicuous a place in the System of Counterfeit Christianity he has promulgated in his " Orthodox and Catholic Doctrine of our Lord's Human Nature," that it demands more space, in order to expose its delusive and destructive tendency, than can be allotted to a mere Note to this part of the Letter. It is my design, therefore, to notice this subject of Holiness, amongst others, more at large in the Postscript; wherein I shall attempt to shew, from *Mr. Irving's* own statements, that he first *denies* the scriptural Account of it, and then sets up his own " wretched, soul-destroying Error," instead of it. In so doing he " forsakes the Fountain of Living Waters, and hews out to himself Cisterns, broken Cisterns, that can hold no Water," as the following quotations, amongst others, will abundantly prove.

" For certain (he says) CHRIST had a Body and Soul of Man's Substance, without thereby having a *Human* PERSON: and *therefore,* WE CAN ASSERT the *Sinfulness* of the *whole*, the *complete*, the *perfect Human Nature* which He took, *without* in *the least* implicating HIM with *Sin!*" (*Pref.* x.)

" It doth not make HIM a *Sinner* that HE took *Sinful Flesh*, any more than that HE came into a *Sinful World*, and *departed into Death*. I SAY HE took *Sin-FUL* Flesh, and yet was *Sin-LESS*; and, moreover, I SAY, that He died, and yet was *Sinless*. If any man say that this is a mere matter of Words, I tell him he hath yet to learn the *Alphabet* of his Theology." (pa. 86.) " To know and to understand *how* the SON OF GOD took *Sin-FUL* Flesh, and yet was *Sin-LESS*, (he tells us on pa. 18.) is the *Alpha* and the *Omega*, the *Beginning* and the *Ending* of Orthodox *Theology!*"

In such ways as these, it is, that *Mr. Irving* " sacrifices to his own Net, and burns Incense to his own Drag:" exclaiming, as he does, on pa. 49, (after having set forth in the preceding one his own delusive views of Reconciliation or Atonement by the supposed agreement between the *unholy Will* of *his Christ's Sinful Manhood*, and the *holy Will* of His GODHEAD;") " WHAT *Reconciliation* like THIS RECONCILIATION? WHAT *At-one-ment* like THIS AT-ONE-MENT?" And because others *dare not* presume to embrace his Errors, and *will not* assert with him that CHRIST's Flesh was " *Sinful* Flesh *as ours,*

And as to the *Atonement*—that great, and gracious, and glorious Doctrine of divine Revelation—it is truly grievous, yea, *very* grievous indeed to me, and to many, to see how *Mr. Irving's* Sentiments would first pervert, and then destroy it !*  The derisive manner in which he speaks on pp. 442, 443, of what may be considered a scriptural account of it, as a Satisfaction to offended Justice, as a Reconciliation

---

" with the *same Dispositions,* and *Propensities,* and *Wants,* and *Afflictions,*" he hesitates not to declare that " GOD hath sent such Men *strong Delusion,* that they should believe a *Lie !*" (pa. 23.)  But what saith the *Scriptures ?* " For we have not an High Priest which cannot be touched with the feeling of our Infirmities, but was in all points tempted like as we are, yet WITHOUT SIN," *Heb.* iv. 15.  " FOR SUCH an High Priest *became* US, who is HOLY, HARMLESS, UNDEFILED, SEPARATE FROM SINNERS, and made higher than the Heavens; For the *Law* maketh *Men* High Priests which *have* INFIRMITY ; but the *Word of the Oath* which was *since* the Law, (or rather " *beyond* the Law," as μετα is here rendered by *Dr. Doddridge,* and is approved by *Mr. Parkhurst,* who very justly observes, that " AFTER *the Law,* plainly relates not to the time when the *Oath* was *made,* but to that in which it was to *take effect ;*"—and *beyond,* or *on the other side,* is evidently the meaning of μετα in *Heb.* ix. 3: Thus, " the WORD *of the* OATH which was *beyond,* or *prior to* the Law,) maketh THE SON, who is *consecrated for evermore !*"                *Heb.* vii. 26, 28.

* " Branding the *Truth* with the name of *Heresy,*" *Mr. Irving* " dare not but seem to be Orthodox," and therefore he occasionally quotes a " form of sound words" from the Church of *Scotland,* and sometimes even from the Holy Scriptures themselves ; when his own Interpretations and Explanations clearly shew that he applies a very different meaning to the terms used.  In this way *Mr. Irving* may be said to " hold the truth in unrighteousness"—not, indeed, in unrighteousness of *Life,* but in unrighteousness of *Interpretation !* And, in so doing, he becomes much more dangerous to the weak in Faith than the avowed Enemy, who openly maintains his opposition to the Truth without assuming its garb.  That he evidently perverts, and then destroys, the glorious Doctrine of the *Atonement,* which he nevertheless professes to believe and maintain, is not only apparent from the above Quotations and Interpretations from " *The Morning Watch,*" (in which that Doctrine is set forth, 1st, " as the *Reconciliation* of the *Sinful* Will of *Christ's* sinful Manhood to His GOD-HEAD," and 2ndly, as the *Redemption* of his *Human Will* out of Bondage by the power of His *Divine*) but also from the passages that follow from " The Orthodox Doctrine ;" each of which sets forth the *Atonement* in unscriptural Language, an unscriptural Thing.

In pa. 99, he says, " Atonement and Redemption are the names for the bearing of CHRIST'S WORK *upon* the SINNER ; and have no respect to its bearing upon the GODHEAD, nor upon *The Christ* the GOD-MAN."

In *Pref.* vii. To understand the *Work* which our LORD did, you must understand the *Materials* with which He did it.  The *Work* which He did was to *reconcile,* sanctify, quicken, and glorify *this Nature* of ours, which is *full* of Sin, and *Death,* and *Rebellion,* and *Dishonour* unto GOD."

In pa. 88, If it (the Atonement) be, as the *English* word plainly imports,

made to God for the Sins of His People—and as a Redemption by *Price*—shews how wide He is from any real acquaint-
ance with the Truth " as it is in Jesus:" for, instead of
any scriptural account of the Atonement, he sets up his own
fanciful description of a *supposed Redemption* of a sinful
*human Will* by the mere operation, or energizing, of *Divine
Power*—and *that* Redemption, too, is made to consist of the

---

the Condition of being *at one* with God; then there is no such Atonement
wrought, or promised, or exhibited *as done in* Christ, unless He did join in
personal union, and harmony, and oneness, for ever, the two several and sepa-
rated and discordant things; namely, the *Nature* of God, and the *Nature* of the
*Apostate Sinful Creature.*"  " If His Human Nature differed, by however little,
from ours, in its *Alienation* and *Guiltiness*, then the work of reducing *it* into
eternal harmony with God, hath no bearing whatever upon *our* Nature, with
which it is not *the same.*"  " And as to His having an *un*fallen Nature to bring
into oneness or Reconciliation, the thing is *nonsensical ;* for an *un*fallen Nature, a Will in the state of Creation is at no variance nor Enmity with God, but
his own good and pleasant Workmanship.  This, which is the *natural* Idea of
Atonement, or Reconciliation, hath not only *no reality*, but even not so much
as *a meaning*, upon any other *supposition* than that Christ took our *fallen*
Nature, with all its natural and inherent Propensities; and overcame these,
and brought it into union with Godhead, and hath fixed it there for ever by
the Resurrection."
     In pa. 40, " And thus do you behold in the Resurrection, the Reconcilia-
tion or Atonement accomplished between God and *Man* in the *Person* of the
Lord Jesus Christ, *through* the *union* of the Godhead to *fallen Humanity*."
     In pa. 100, " Thus have I shewn, that, looking at the *Atonement* how you
please, it not only doth not fall, but *standeth*, in the *fact* that Christ *took
Human Nature in the fallen state !*"
     Here it will be observed, that in no one of the quotations given, has *Mr.
Irving* represented the *Atonement* as it is spoken of in the Book of God;
namely, as an " Atonement by Blood"—as a " Reconciliation for Iniquity"—
as a *Ransom* to God for the Sins of His People, " by the precious Blood of
Christ, as of a Lamb without blemish and without spot;" but by his unscriptural statements he perverts it, and in effect destroys it; as we shall see by a
careful examination of the Quotations that have been just exhibited, and of the
Observations that follow.  In pa. 99, he informs us, that the true Atonement is
not that which " continues to be *doated on* by the *Church*," but that " Atonement and Redemption are the names for the bearing of Christ's *Work* upon the
*Sinner*"—and that " to understand the *Work* which our Lord did, you must
understand the *Materials* with which He did it"—(*Pref.* vii.)  Three Subjects
here present themselves for our consideration : the *Worker*—the *Materials*—
and the *Work*.  And of each a few Thoughts in the order mentioned.
     1. *The Worker*.  This, we are told, in *Pref.* x. is " Christ"—in *Pref.* vii.
" our Lord"—in *Pref.* x. the " *Person* of the Son of God"—and in pp. 98, 131,
" God."  Or in other words, the *Divine* Nature of Christ—for thus we read in
pa. 2, " I believe that my Lord did *come down*, and toil, and sweat, and travail, in
exceeding great sorrow, in this Mass of Temptation (or Iniquity, as it is in *Mor.
Watch*, 421.) with which I and every sinful man are oppressed; did *bring* His

*Almighty Power* of CHRIST's *Divine* Nature subduing or re-straining, "every variety of Human Wickedness" within HIS OWN *Human* Nature! Or, in other words, redeeming *His own Human Will* from the *Bondage* of "a Nature," (His own *sinful Humanity*) "which drew it away from GOD, and was, of itself, rebellious against GOD!" For, *this* he declares "is *what* the SON OF GOD *did*," (or, as he there

---

*Divine Person* into Death-possessed Humanity, into the one Substance of Man-kind created in *Adam*, and by the Fall brought into a state of resistance to and alienation from GOD, of Condemnation and proclivity to Evil, of Subjection to the *Devil*."—In pa. 131, " I want proof of His GODHEAD in His action; and I have shewn thee how I get it, by seeing His Creature Nature, the World, and the Devil, all set against HIM, and something *in* Him prevailing *against* adverse Creation; which thing I thereby know to be *not* Creation, but the very contrary of a fallen Creation—GOD." In pa. 98, he says, " It is GOD who *doth* the thing." From these Statements, it is evident, that the *Worker* is the GODHEAD of CHRIST, considered " *apart* from" that *Nature* (His " *Sinful Manhood*") in which the *Work* was done.

2. *The Materials.* These are shewn to be the *sinful Body* and *sinful Soul* of *Mr. Irving's Christ;* INTO which (the preceding quotation from pa. 2. in-forms us) CHRIST's *Divine* Person CAME; and *in* which (or " *on*," " *upon*," or " *with* which," as at other places) His *Divine* Person " did the Work." These Materials—the *inherently Sinful Manhood* of *his* Christ—Mr. Irving calls, amongst other things, " this Nature of ours, which is *full* of *Sin*, and *Death*, and *Rebellion*, and *Dishonour* unto GOD"—Humanity in which *every variety* of Human *Wickedness* was inherent, and *combined* against *divine Holi-ness*—17. "the Nature of the *Apostate Sinful Creature*"—" our *fallen* Nature, with all its *natural* and *inherent Propensities*"—(88.) " GOD's own *sunken, ruined Creation*"—(31.) " *Death-possessed Humanity*—the one *Substance* of *Manhood* created in *Adam*, and by the Fall brought into a state of *resistance to*, and *alienation* from GOD, of *condemnation* and *proclivity* to *Evil*, of *subjec-tion* to the *Devil*"—(2.) His own Flesh that " carried up to *Him* every form of Seduction"—(26.) In a word, that desperate wicked Manhood with which *Mr. Irving* says, " the SON OF MAN was clothed upon withal," and which, in pa. 126, he describes as " *corrupt* to the *very heart's core*, and from the *centre* of its *inmost Will* sending forth Streams *black* as *Hell*"—"*bristling thick* and *strong* with *Sin* like the *hairs* upon the *Porcupine!*"

3. *The Work.* This, though somewhat differently described in different places, uniformly amounts to this: the *energy* of the *Divine* Nature of CHRIST or of the SPIRIT, so *subduing* His inherently *sinful Human* Nature, as to bring it into *subjection* thereto, without the smallest possible change from Sin to Holi-ness having been wrought *in* the *Human* Nature, either by its union to the *Di-vine*, or by the Indwelling of the HOLY GHOST—or by any Operation whatever!

In *Pref.* vii. we are told, that, " The Work which He (our LORD) did, was to *reconcile*, sanctify, quicken and glorify *this* Nature of *ours*, which is *full* of Sin, and Death, and Rebellion, and Dishonour unto GOD." In pa. 80, that " He was conscious to the *native* and natural *Unholiness*, Alienation and Rebellion of *it*," (the very Nature He assumed) " and in that consciousness entered on the *perilous Work* of redeeming and reclaiming it." " *His Creature-*

means, the *Divine Nature* of CHRIST,) and *this* was the WHOLE of what CHRIST did in FLESH," pa. 432 ; and which, in his own unscriptural Phraseology, *Mr. Irving* calls "fallen Human Nature subdued unto Holiness, made obedient to the Law of GOD ! ! !"

In page 435, *Mr. Irving* informs us, that the Word *"Atonement"* or Reconciliation, is of *"rare"* occurrence,

---

*nature"* being *"part* and *parcel* of the *fallen* and *rebellious* Creation, in reconciling *which* He reconciled *all."* (*Pref.* viii.)   In pa. 40, this Work is called a " reconciling unto GOD the *inveterate Obstinacy* and *stubborn Rebellion* of *Flesh* and *Blood."*   In pa. 18, "GODHEAD contending against SIN in *Flesh."* In pa. 86, " GOD overcoming  Sin in that estate (CHRIST's Sinful Flesh)." " CHRIST's *Flesh* being the fit Field of Contention, because *it* is the *same* on which *Satan* hath *triumphed* ever since the Fall." " *Here,* then, in the *Flesh* of CHRIST is the *great Controversy waged."* And which Flesh is there described as *"fit,* because it was linked unto all material things, *Devil-possessed."*   In pa. 88, this work is called, " the work of *reducing* it (CHRIST's " Human Nature which differed not  from ours, by however little, in its Alienation and Guiltiness") into *eternal harmony* with GOD !"   In pa. 89, " The *Person* of the *Word* taking a Human Will, under those very Bondages into union with *Himself;* and, *acting therein,* did *deliver it* completely out of all those *Oppressions* of the *Devil,* the *World,* and the *Flesh"*— which Work in pa. 67, is described as " overcoming with the weakness and penury (of His Flesh) the utmost might of the *Devil."* For " such *Power* of *Holiness* hath GOD (he says in pa. 67) that *with* the weak Instruments of *fallen Humanity* (CHRIST's Sinful Human Nature,) He did combat and cast the *Devil* out," even out of CHRIST's " Sinful Flesh." And in pa. 88, we read, " This, which is the *natural* Idea of Atonement, or Reconciliation, hath not only no *reality,* but even not so much as *a meaning,* upon *any other supposition* than that CHRIST took our *fallen* Nature, with *all* its *natural* and *inherent Propensities;* and *overcame these,* and brought IT into *union* with GODHEAD, and hath fixed IT there for ever by the Resurrection."

From these Authorities, it appears, that *Mr. Irving* makes the *Divine* Nature of *his Christ* to reconcile, or to atone for His *Human* Nature ! Which is, in fact, not only to make CHRIST to be *" divided,"* but even to maintain that *one part* atoned for that very same *part* of HIMSELF—or else, that the *Human* Nature was *no part* of *Mr. Irving's Christ.*   According to the above Quotations, we find *The Worker,* in *Mr. Irving's* Atonement, evidently shewn to be the GODHEAD of the LORD JESUS CHRIST : — *The Materials* with which He did the work—His " *Sinful Manhood :"*—And the WORK done—the *Reconciliation* of *such Manhood* unto GOD !   Such also being the substance (though in other words expressed) of the above Quotations referred to in *The Mor. Watch*—the Redemption of the *Sinful* Human Will which He took, " from the Bondage of a *Nature* which *drew it away from* GOD, and was of itself *rebellious against* GOD :" this was " verily *what* HE did, and *this* was the WHOLE of what HE did *in Flesh."* (87.)

Aware that his own statement of the Reconciliation would be objected to, on the grounds that it made CHRIST to work out a Righteousness for the very

yea, "of *very* rare occurrence in Scripture"—and therefore he thinks proper to substitute *another* term for it, namely, *Redemption*—(a very suspicious circumstance this, when Men will substitute other terms for the LORD's.\*) Whereas this very word "Atonement" is expressly used between *twenty* and *thirty* times, at the least, in the Holy Scriptures, as every one may see by turning to a good Concordance; and is repeated no less than *eight times* in *one chapter*, (the 16th, of *Leviticus*,) in which we have so blessed an account of the great day of Atonement, GOD's everlasting Statute in *Israel*,—until the great Atoning Sacrifice should come "to put away Sin by the Sacrifice of Himself." In which chapter we have not a single Sentence that will in the smallest degree sanction *Mr. Irving's* fanciful view of Atonement, (namely, as a redemption of Man's Will, or a bringing of *Man's sinful* Will into union with GOD's *holy* Will, through CHRIST's having a Will just as sinful as Man's) but we have GOD's account of an *Atonement* by BLOOD—of *Reconciliation* made to GOD *for* the *Iniquity* of *His People*—"for without shedding of *Blood* there is no Remission"—"for it is the *Blood* that maketh an Atonement for the Soul." But *Mr. Irving's* Atonement, (or rather Redemption, since he appears not to

---

Nature He took, as well as to *atone* for it, (95, 87.) *Mr. Irving* replies to the Objector, on pa. 87, " Thou blunderest in making His *Nature* a PERSON." Whereas it is *Mr. Irving Himself* who blunders, in making only the *Divine* Nature of CHRIST to constitute the *Person* of CHRIST, as before shewn ; and on that account he presumes to assert with impunity, the " Sinfulness of the whole *Human* Nature which CHRIST took, without in the least implicating HIM with *Sin*," (*Pref.* x.) But so long as CHRIST'S Human Nature be considered *inherently Sinful*, and *Sin* be defined, as it is in pa. 38, " any *want* of *Conformity to*, or Transgression of, the Law of GOD," *Mr. Irving's Christ* must be considered *a Sinner*, according to His own shewing—the Nature that He took also stood in need of an *Atonement*—and of the shedding and application of *other Blood* than its own, in order to cleanse it from *all* Sin ; because he assures us that " every variety of Human Wickedness was inherent in His Humanity." And CHRIST being thus made a *Sinner*, " all Creeds (to use *Mr. Irving's* words,) were then at an end, and all Churches ;" and those who thus make CHRIST a Sinner, " were worthy to die the death of Blasphemers, to be stoned by the multitude in the open face of Day." *Ortho. Doc.* pa. 2.

\* All the Words of WISDOM, (we are assured) " are plain to him that understandeth, and right to them that find knowledge," *Prov.* viii. 9. But that precious Word, *Atonement*, does *not* seem *right* to *Mr. Irving*—and why ? But because he has not found the *knowledge* referred to in the above Text.

like the scriptural *term* there used, because, in truth, he likes not the scriptural *Doctrine*,) *Mr. Irving's* Atonement, or Redemption, is *not* an *Atonement* by BLOOD—it is *no Reconciliation* to GOD for Iniquity—it is *no Ransom* given to GOD for the Life of Man—it is no *Satisfaction* to divine Justice through the "*Blood* of the *Cross*"—it is *no Redemption* by *Price*, even by the "precious Blood of CHRIST;" "as of a Lamb without blemish and without spot"—for, in pa. 441, *Mr. Irving* states, that "the Person of the SON OF GOD presented His *Creature* Will, sustained against all visible, sensible oppositions, in perfect Harmony with the Will of GOD"—"and is *this* ALL?" *Mr. Irving* asks—"*This* IS ALL," he immediately answers—and in pa. 432, he says, and *this* was the WHOLE of "what He (CHRIST) did in *Flesh*." Thus, while the Holy Scriptures use the Word "Atonement," and make much, yea, every thing of the *Blood* of the atoning Sacrifice, as to "Reconciliation for Iniquity," *Mr. Irving* likes not the Term—substitutes another—and so leaves the Thing altogether, for the counterfeit Atonement of his own Fancy! For where does he say even one word of "the *Blood* that makes the Atonement for the Soul," in any of the pages I have so largely referred to in this Letter?

No wonder, then, that *Mr. Irving* should say, as he does, pa. 439, that he differs "widely"—"*very* widely"—"very widely *indeed*," from Views "held by many otherwise Orthodox Men upon these subjects"—differing so very widely as he does from the Scriptures of Truth—and although he says "he *perceives* these things, in his own mind, *clearly* and distinctly, and has reflected much thereon," I must confess I never read such confused, contradictory, and unscriptural Statements on any subject in Divinity, as those contained in this very Production of his "On the *True* Humanity of CHRIST!"

To shew how little *Mr. Irving* approves of the scriptural account of the Doctrine of the Atonement, (a Doctrine which lies at the very foundation of the Saints' Jubilee on earth, and their eternal rejoicing in heaven,) I must remind my honoured friend of what *Mr. Irving* has said in pp. 442, 443, under that head. He there calls such statement of the Doctrine, "the Stock-jobbing Theology of the religious

World!"*—"that God wanted Punishment, and an infinite amount of it, for Man's Sin"—"Stripe for Stripe—Suffering for Suffering—which Christ endured for *so many*, and so God is satisfied, and *they* escape from His Anger, which flames as hot as ever against *all beyond this Pale!*"—the Atonement "not being necessary," he states, "to *make* God *placable*," as some say, " for He is *Love* already, and always;"—"not to drain off His Rage, as you represent it, for He is *Merciful* already."    But what has become of God's Justice, all this while, in *Mr. Irving's* esteem? What does he with those alarming Declarations of the "Spirit of Holiness" in "the Scriptures of Truth," "the Soul that sinneth it shall die!"—"Cursed is every one that continueth not in all things that are written in the Book of the Law, to

---

* Of all the various ways by which *Mr. Irving* shews his opposition to "the Truth as it is in Jesus," his calling the Atonement in Christ's Blood "the *Stock-jobbing Theology* of the Religious World," and those who advocate it, "*Brokers* who cry up *their own* Article," (96.) are not amongst the least offensive to the true Believer in the Son of God. Whatever might have been the precise object *Mr. Irving* had in view, in making these and similar assertions, it is evident to those "who are spiritual," that, however *Mr. Irving* may sometimes use the *Terms*, yet that he really denies the *Doctrines* of the *Suretyship* of Jesus, of the *Imputation* of Sin, and the *Imputation of Righteousness* also; since he pretends to make out that the Sin of the Church was imPARted to a part of Christ—His *Human Nature* only — instead of being imputed to Him, the God-man, who was *ever inherently holy* in His Human Nature, although, as the *Surety* of His People, He became as legally responsible to Divine Justice for all their Sins as if He had personally committed every one of them. Thus, in pa. 123, *Mr. Irving* complains of "logical Fictions," being substituted for "Theological Truths," "by the representation of Christ as a *Substitute merely*, as one having things imputed *to* Him, but *not* imPARted to Him ;" the *divine transfer* of the *Sin* of the *Church* to Christ, and of His Righteousness to the *Church*, being what *Mr. Irving* derides in those words, the "Stock-jobbing Theology of the Religious World." In which gracious and glorious Work, the Almighty Three in Jehovah, the Father, the Word, and the Holy Ghost, are, in truth, the Persons reproached as the "Brokers;" (*Luke* x. 16.) for *they*, and *they only* have effected this wonderful Transfer, however *Mr. Irving* may attempt to oppose it, to confound it, to despise it, to reject it! (*Isa.* liii. 6. 2 *Cor.* v. 21.)

In setting forth the Sin of the Church as imPARted to, or *inherent in* Christ, instead of being imputed *to or put upon* Him, *Mr. Irving* reverses the very order of things exhibited in the Scriptures, and falls into the very absurdity of which *Mr. Romaine* speaks in the Note given on pa. 3, in reference to the *Types*, as follows :—" All the Sins of the Children of *Israel* were *passed over to* the Goat, (*Lev.* xvi. 21.) but were they *put into* the Goat, or were they *inherent* in him? No : *this is too absurd to be supposed :* but they were *put upon* the Goat." And

do them!" Surely *Mr. Irving* forgets that GOD must be infinitely *just* to all the holy Requirements, to all the righteous Denunciations, of His holy, just, and righteous Law, before He can manifest infinite *Mercy* to a miserable Transgressor! And that GOD's love of *Justice* is full as great as His Love of *Mercy*—since both are Infinite; and between things Infinite there is no disparity! And that GOD delights to manifest his Infinite Mercy to His People through divine Satisfaction to His Infinite Justice—The Sword having been pleased to awake against His Shepherd, as His People's Surety, and to smite the *Head* of the Church that all the *Members* might go free; for thus it is written, *Zech.* xiii. 7, "Awake, O Sword, against My Shepherd, against the MAN *my Fellow*, saith the LORD of HOSTS, smite the Shepherd, and the

---

yet into this very absurdity, with respect to the ANTITYPE, *Mr. Irving's* Doctrine unavoidably leads him, since he maintains, that " *That* HOLY THING," which was " conceived in," and " born of" " the Virgin," and which is so expressly declared to have been " OF the HOLY GHOST," (*Matt.* i. 18, 20.) had " every variety of *Human Wickedness* INHERENT *in it!*" The typical Scape-Goat, we know, had not any *one* Sin of Israel *impARted* to him so as to be inherent in him, but had *all* their *Iniquities* put *upon* him, and for which the slain Goat was sacrificed. And yet *Mr. Irving* hesitates not to assert, that " the *Atonement* standeth in the *fact* that CHRIST took Human Nature in the *fallen* state," (pa. 100.) Whereas, those who have indeed " received the Atonement" by the Revelation of the HOLY GHOST, know that it would be completely destroyed if such pretended fact were true. And equally false is that other statement of his, on pa. 151, that " those who ignorantly and heretically maintain that CHRIST took UN*fallen* Flesh, or that in its Conception His Flesh was brought into a different Law of Being from ours, can give no Account of His Death whatever, so as to justify GOD." How then came the inherently Sinless Goat to die? or the LORD " to bruise Him who was led as a *Lamb* to the slaughter;" " who did no violence, neither was any deceit found in His mouth;" nor had any Sin inherent in His Nature, because He was "holy, harmless, undefiled, and separate from Sinners ;" and so lived and died, " the just for the unjust," and thus " restored that which *He* took not away."?

That *Mr. Irving's* sentiments would destroy the precious *Suretyship* of JESUS, I refer to pa. 113, where he in substance declares, that if CHRIST's Human Nature had not been just as *inherently sinful* as ours, He could not have been our *Substitute*. But who besides *Mr. Irving* ever considered that the *very thing* that *disqualifies* the *Principal* for service, should be the very thing that *qualifies* His *Substitute?* Or, that in order to become an *available* SURETY, it were an *indispensable Prerequisite* that the Person so engaging should be just as incapable of paying the Creditor as the Bankrupt-debtor himself? For, *Mr. Irving's Christ*, with an *inherently Sinful* Nature, could no more *be holy*, or *act righteously*, as the holy and righteous Law of GOD requires, than *Mr. Irving* himself can. And all his Sophistry in setting forth the *counterfeit Holiness* and *Righteousness* of the false *Christ* he sets up,

Sheep shall be scattered abroad"—" Yet it pleased the LORD to bruise *Him!*"—" But *He* was wounded for *our* Transgressions, *He* was bruised for *our* Iniquities; the chastisement of *our* Peace was upon *Him;* and with *His* Stripes *we* are healed." "For CHRIST hath redeemed us from the Curse of the Law, being made a Curse for us," *Isa.* liii. 10. with *Gal.* iii. 13. But *Mr. Irving* sets up *his Reason* as the standard, then neglects the Word, and ultimately rejects the Doctrine, of " the Scriptures of Truth:" for they have repeatedly used the term " Atonement," which he does not like—and they have expressly declared that *Messiah* should come " to make Reconciliation for Iniquity"—*which* Reconciliation *Mr. Irving,* by his statements, considers entirely unnecessary; since he says " GOD was *Love always;*" " GOD

without a *purity* of *Nature,* will avail him no more at the Bar of Divine *Justice,* than the Thoughts, Words, and Works, of the *Second Adam,* with the Sinful Nature that he possessed, availed *him* when the voice of the LORD GOD called unto him in the Garden, " Where art thou ?" *Gen.* iii. 9.

In pa. 75, *Mr. Irving* says, that Suffering could not reach an *un*-fallen Creature, and therefore, that CHRIST *must* have had a *fallen* Nature, or he *could not* have *suffered;* although the Scriptures assure us, that " CHRIST *hath* once suffered for Sins, the *just* for the *unjust,* that He might bring us to GOD," (1 *Pet.* iii. 18.) And although he says his Opponents " do indeed talk long and loud about its being *vicarious* and *sacrificial* to cleanse away our Sins, which (he adds) no Orthodox Man ever denied,"—yet, he continues, " if CHRIST's Flesh were *unfallen* Flesh, *how* could it *die* without GOD's violating the Law of Creation, which is not Death, but Life ?" To which must be added, from pa. 116, " The Man who will put a Fiction, whether Legal or Theological, a *make believe* into his Ideas of GOD, *I have done with;* he who will make GOD consider a Person to be that which *he is not,* and act towards him *as* that which he is not, *I have done with.* That if CHRIST was *not* in the *Condition* of the Sinner, and GOD treated Him as if He had been so; if *that* be the meaning of THEIR *Imputation* and *Substitution,* or by whatever name they call it, AWAY WITH IT, AWAY WITH IT from MY *Theology* FOR EVER !"

In all these quotations *Mr. Irving* " leans to his *own* understanding," and so errs, not knowing the Scriptures by the Power of GOD. For, had he indeed known them by that " demonstration of the SPIRIT," of which the Apostle speaks in 1 *Cor.* ii. 4, his Words would not have been " stout against the Lord," as they have been, to the destruction of his own Soul's Faith and Hope, in the very Anathemas he has pronounced on others. Let us only examine the last Quotation given, from pa. 116, " He who will make GOD consider a Person to be *that* which *he is not,* and act towards him *as* that which he *is not,* I HAVE DONE WITH !" Then, in the *first* place, *Mr. Irving* must have done with *Himself;* for he declares in pa. 86, 117, that although CHRIST was *not* a Sinner, yet GOD treated Him as if he *had been* a Sinner ! In the *second* place, *Mr. Irving* must have done with the " Scriptures of Truth," for their uniform Testimony is, that the LORD's CHRIST " knew no Sin," and that he " did no Sin," neither

was *Merciful already!*" It was *Iniquity,* however, for which Reconciliation or Atonement was required to be made, and *was* made; and not merely a *Bond-will* to be redeemed, as *Mr. Irving* fancies and asserts. *To whom* was this Reconciliation to be made? but to Him against whom the Iniquity was committed—even to GOD! And *how* was this to be effected? but by the precious Blood of the "holy, harmless, Lamb of GOD," who was delivered for our Offences and raised again for our Justification"—it being the Blood that maketh the "Atonement for the Soul"— "without the shedding of which there is no "Remission"— and it is the blood of CHRIST alone that speaks in the believing Sinner's Conscience, through the operation of the HOLY GHOST, the Peace it has made with GOD for the Sin of

---

was Guile found in His Mouth;" yet that "it pleased the LORD to bruise Him!" and to "put Him to Grief,"—"the just for the unjust." He having become the *Surety* of us Strangers, was made to smart for our Offences. And in the *third* place, *Mr. Irving* must have done even with GOD HIMSELF! for *He* it is who laid upon the Spotless Lamb of GOD, "the Iniquities of us all;" who was "wounded for our Transgressions, and bruised for our Iniquities: the Chastisement of our peace was laid upon Him, and with His Stripes we are healed," *Isa.* liii. 6. After these annihilations, *Mr. Irving* must of course have done with that precious Doctrine which is after GOD, and according to Godliness,— the *Imputation* of the *Sin* of the Church to CHRIST, and of *His Righteousness* to the *Church;* especially since he declares in pa. 116, that "If CHRIST was *not* in the *Condition* of the Sinner, ("the *very* Condition," as in pa. 117, and by which he means just as *inherently sinful* as the Sinner, 22.) and GOD treated Him as if He *had* been so, if *this* be *their* Imputation and Substitution, &c. "AWAY WITH IT, AWAY WITH IT from MY *Theology* FOR EVER!" In this fearful rejection, *Mr. Irving* at once and for ever casts away the very Foundation of the *Christian Ministry,* and all the *Christian's Hope,* which is set before us in these precious words: "For HE hath made *Him* who *knew no Sin,* to be *Sin* for *us,* that *we* might be made the *Righteousness* of GOD in *Him!*" 2 *Cor.* v. 21. The *inherently Sinless Sacrifice* is, by Divine Imputation, made His People's *Sin;* and they, though Sinners in themselves, are, by the same gracious Imputation, made *Righteous,* even the RIGHTEOUSNESS OF GOD in HIM—"Who of GOD is made unto them Wisdom, and Righteousness, and Sanctification, and Redemption: that according as it is written, He that glorieth, let him glory in the LORD," 1 *Cor.* i. 30, 31.

*Mr. Irving* may therefore continue to *despise* that precious fundamental Doctrine of *Divine* IMPUTATION, calling it as he does, "the *poisonous Garment* of the *popular Theology,*"—"the Stock-jobbing Theology of the Religious World," &c. and he may disdainfully *reject* it, as he does, in calling it "*their* Imputation:" of which he exclaims, "Away with it, away with it from *my* Theology for ever!" because *it* militates against that "wild Hypothesis and most fearful Error" of his, the *inherent Sinfulness* of the Humanity of JESUS: or, he may even profess to *espouse* it, as he does, on pa. 117, where he tells us, "It is

his Soul. It is "in Him," therefore, even in the LORD's
CHRIST, as the Apostle says, that "WE have Redemption,"
even "*through* HIS Blood." Of *this* Redemption the Saints
in *Heaven* sing, "THOU hast redeemed *us to* GOD by THY
BLOOD." For, saith the Apostle, in that verse before
quoted, (*Gal.* iii. 13.) "CHRIST hath redeemed *us* from the
curse of the Law, being made a *Curse* for *us.*" GOD declares
that "He is *pacified*" towards His People—"Mercy and
Truth having met together, Righteousness and Peace having
kissed each other," in the Person and Sacrifice of the LORD
JESUS CHRIST. But of *this Atonement* by the *Blood* of the
Cross of CHRIST, or of the *Peace* of GOD brought into the
Conscience by the Power of the HOLY GHOST, we read no
more in *Mr. Irving's* Treatise than if they never had existence in any part of GOD's holy Word, or in the Hearts of His
regenerated, justified, sanctified People.*

---

*Substitution*, that CHRIST from being the SON of GOD should *instead thereof*
become the *Son of Man.*" But of *such* a Substitution as *this* of his, the essential
GODHEAD of CHRIST *put in the place* of His *sinful* MANHOOD, (for it *is* Substitution, he informs us, " that CHRIST from being the SON of GOD should
INSTEAD THEREOF become the *Son* of MAN,") thus changing the very PERSON
of CHRIST, annihilating His very GODHEAD, and leaving only His *Sinful Manhood* by the change! Of such a delusive Substitution as this, we may truly say
what he does of the scriptural one which he rejects, that it is a " destructive
Falsehood," fabricated out of the Truth, by the ingenuity of *Satan*, and the
perversity of Men." (117.)

So deeply does *Mr. Irving* appear to have drank of the intoxicating con-
tents of the " Cup of *Error*," that, in the estimation of some, he stands a conspicuous Way-mark in the Professing Church of the Nineteenth Century, with
this Soul-humbling record inscribed thereon : " *Man* by WISDOM KNOWS *not*
GOD !" The Altar where he worships bearing that *Athenian* Inscription—" To
THE UNKNOWN GOD."

* "But a *very poor Wit* have they, and a *most barbarous Idea* of GOD,"
(*Mr. Irving* informs us in pa. 98,) who will represent this sublime, stupendous
Action of GODHEAD as taking place in order to appease the *Wrath* of GODHEAD,
which verily takes place to manifest the Love and Grace and Mercy of GOD-
HEAD." And this he declares, because *he* doth " so nauseate and repudiate
the *true* Doctrine of the *Atonement;* which Doctrine, in pa. 101, he calls " the
System of Theology with which the Evangelical part of the Church are nou-
rished, or rather *poisoned*,"—and in pa. 102, " the *poisonous* Garment of the
*popular Theology*, that GOD *loveth Suffering*, and will have it out of some one
or other without Abatement"—" Stripe for Stripe, Suffering for Suffering," (96.)
—" that GOD *wanteth Punishment*, and an infinite Amount of it ; which CHRIST
gave for *so many;* and so *He* is *satisfied*, and *they escape* from His *Anger*,
which flames as hot as ever against *all beyond this Pale*," (95.) All this, and
much more than this, *Mr. Irving* asserts, in order to oppose " the Idea," as he
calls that which is in truth the very *Essence* or *Substance* of the Atonement,

How daring then is it for any one to speak of the Doctrine of the *Atonement* as *Mr. Irving* does, and call it " the Stock-jobbing Theology of the religious World," &c., and of all those venerable Fathers in the Church who have supported what he rejects, (and before whom, as a Divine, *Mr. Irving* shines but as an expiring Taper before the mid-day Sun) as "Brokers, crying up their own article"—"which will not do"—when *Mr. Irving* says *Nothing* of that *only* Atonement *by Blood*, of which the *Scriptures* say so much —and *he* says *so much* of the redemption of a Bond-will *in* CHRIST'S *human* Nature, by the Power of His *Divine;* of which Redemption, (falsely so called) the Scriptures say *Nothing!* *Mr. Irving's* Redemption, too, is *one universal* Redemption of *all* Mankind—the *Love* of GOD being applied by him " to *every one* of the Family of Mankind"—(445.) the *Righteousness* of CHRIST declared to be " universal."—The

---

namely, Satisfaction to the punitive Justice of GOD by the death of CHRIST, in the stead, and for the Sins, of His chosen People. For, " *Atonement* and *Redemption,*" he asserts, " are the Names for the bearing of CHRIST'S Work upon the *Sinner;* and have *no respect* to its bearing upon the GODHEAD, nor upon CHRIST the GOD-MAN," (99.)—and that " while the *present* views of the *Atonement* continued to be *doated on* by the Church, it is in vain to attempt to carry any point of *sound* Doctrine!" (99.) Or rather, as the Truth is—while the present views of the Atonement as a Satisfaction to GOD'S Justice for the Sins of His People, continue to be known and enjoyed " by the HOLY GHOST given to them," it is in vain for *Mr. Irving* to think of " imposing on them his own Inventions for the Truth of GOD."

While in some places *Mr. Irving* sets forth the fancied Holiness of *his Christ* without any *inherent purity* or sinlessness of *Nature*, (Pref. x.) and in others, he speaks of a *Righteousness* of CHRIST wrought *in*, or *upon*, or *by* Flesh that " ever loved the Temptation, and ever conversed with the Tempter" —we here find him exhibiting an *Atonement* for Sin, as "the Name" of something that has " *no respect whatever* to any bearing upon the GODHEAD," (against which Sin was committed,) but is the name for the bearing of CHRIST'S work upon the *Sinner!* Such work of CHRIST being described by *Mr. Irving*, as before shewn in the Note on pa. 70, as the power of His own *Divine* Nature *acting on* his *own Sinful Human* Nature, both in a way of RE-*straining* it from indulging in the sinful Propensities it *inherently loved*, and CON-*straining* it to the performance of those holy acts which it *inherently hated*.

And this is called by him, " GODHEAD in *action* towards the *fallen miserable Sinner*"—(102.) And thus his Work of Atonement would even make CHRIST'S Human Nature to be the *Sinner* reconciled, since *that*, in pa. 88, is declared to be at *variance* or enmity with GOD, until it was reconciled to GOD, by the delusive notions *Mr. Irving* has set forth of a *Holiness* without *purity*, and a Righteousness of a Creature in which was inherent " every variety of Human Wickedness!"

" But a very poor Wit, and a most barbarous Idea of GOD," *Mr. Irving* says they must have, who represent this sublime, stupendous action of GODHEAD

*Death* of Christ, "for all men" (445.) and that what He did for *Mr. Irving*, "he did for all the World!" This latter assertion, in one sense, I fear, is, but too true; for, as *Mr. Irving* shews that CHRIST had not done *any thing* to justify *him* by a perfect *Obedience* to the Requirements of the Law; or to redeem *him* from its Condemnation by *suffering* its Curse; or to reconcile *him* to GOD by the Blood of the Cross; or that God declares He is *pacified* towards *him;*" so neither has He done *any thing* of this sort for "*all the World*"—nor, by *Mr. Irving's* own shewing, even for *any single Individual* that ever has lived in it, or ever will! Of course *Mr. Irving* no more maintains the Scripture Doctrine of a *personal Election* by *Grace*, than he does the Scripture Doctrine of a particular *Atonement* by *Blood*. He speaks, it is true, of the Redemption of ALL *Mankind*, yet he says nothing of that DIVINE RANSOM, by which alone any single Soul can be redeemed—THE INESTIMABLY PRE-CIOUS BLOOD OF THE LORD JESUS CHRIST! And although he does just mention the term "Election" on the top of his last page, (445.) "which takes its glorious elevation (he says) from this Basis of *Universal Love*"—yet, notwithstanding "the Death of CHIRST *for all* men," he asserts, "the hatefulness of Sin is shewn out tremendously, the

---

as taking place in order to appease the WRATH of GODHEAD, &c." Such a "very poor wit" then must that Individual have possessed, in whom no incompetent judges have declared that "all the *Majesty* of HOMER," and all the *Gracefulness* of VIRGIL were united—that "Prince of *English* Poets," as he has been called—who has proved, either the poverty of *his* own *Wit*, or of *Mr. Irving's Theology*, in those well known Lines;

"Man, with his whole Posterity must die!
Die *he*, or JUSTICE *must;* unless for him
Some other able, and as willing pay
The *rigid* SATISFACTION—Death for Death!" *Paradise Lost.*

Such a "very barbarous Idea of GOD," too, must that celebrated *English* BISHOP have had, who was styled by his Cotemporaries, ("and not without reason," as *Mr. Hervey* observes,) "*A walking Library*," for he has declared that, "CHRIST, as our *Surety*, paid our *Debts*, underwent the *Curse* due "to our Sins, and representatively in our stead fulfilled all the Righteousness "the Law required, active and passive. For, Sin being once committed, "there must be a double act to *Justification;* the *Suffering* of the *Curse*, "and the *fulfilling* of *Righteousness* anew. The one a *Satisfaction* for the "*Injury* we have done to GOD as our JUDGE; the other, the *Performance* of "a *Service* which we owe unto him as our MAKER."

BISHOP REYNOLDS's *Life of* CHRIST.

nature of Holiness and Justice most awfully, when, *not-withstanding this Love*, GOD *judgeth them to eternal Wrath for the guilt of their Sins!!*" (445).

To pass by all that might be said on the open violence *Mr. Irving* does to all the *Types* which set forth the unspotted *Purity* of the *Nature* of the Sacrifice—and especially the *Paschal Lamb;* which, with all the other Offerings for *Sin*, were so particularly enjoined to be "*without Blemish*," (*Exod.* xii. 5. *Lev.* xxii. 20, 21.—iv. 23, 28, 32.) as typifying the *perfect Purity* of that "LAMB of God, who should be " holy, harmless, undefiled, and separate from Sinners," and who should " put away Sin by the *Sacrifice* of Himself"— I observe, that in pa. 426, he says much in order to make it appear, that CHRIST's *Human* Nature (not being *part* of His *Divine* Person) could not, though sinful in itself, as he asserts, ever constitute CHRIST a *Sinner;*—because Sin, he intimates, never was *in* the *Divine* Nature of CHRIST, nor ever could be committed *by* His *Divine* Nature—such *Divine* Nature *only* (and not the human and divine in union) constituting, in *Mr. Irving's* esteem, the *Person* of the LORD JESUS CHRIST. And as he says Sin is the act of the *Person*, and CHRIST's *Person* was His *Divine* Nature only,

---

Such a " very barbarous Idea of God" also, must that other *English* DI-VINE have possessed, (the distinguished Principal of *St. Mary's Hall*, OXFORD, in 1686,—the Tutor also of many eminent Divines and Scholars in his day, and particularly of the great *Mr. Locke*,) who, on his death-bed, declared to his particular Friend,

" This one thing I am convinced of, that it is foolish to seek for the " *Justification* of a *Sinner* without *Satisfaction* to the *Justice* of GOD ; which " nothing can do but the *Righteousness* of GOD imputed to him. While *Jus-* " *tice* remains *unsatisfied* it will overthrow all other grounds of Hope for " Justification that we can conceive from our own works and doings. The " *Justice* of GOD strikes the Sinner under the Curse, and so leaves him in " a condemned state ; but by the way of CHRIST's *Righteousness* we meet " with no Obstructions. The Devil, the Law, may meet us, yet cannot hin-" der us from entering Heaven. We shall be sure to meet with the Devil, " and Conscience, and wicked Men, and the Law too, in our way to " Heaven, and we can deal with none of them but by that *Righteousness* " that has *satisfied* all. Bring that along with us, and they will all fly be-" fore it. If a Sinner comes in his own Righteousness, ' Shut *him* OUT !' " says GOD, says Conscience, saith the Law, saith the Devil; but when one " comes clothed with the Righteousness of CHRIST, ' Let *him* IN !' saith " GOD, says Conscience, saith the Law. Let the Devil speak a word against " it if he dare !" *Life of the Rev. and learned* THOMAS COLE.

G

which is essentially *holy*, therefore, that CHRIST could not *personally* be a *Sinner*, nor *personally commit* Sin. And thus *Mr. Irving* here also, as in so many other places before mentioned, evidently makes CHRIST's *Human* Nature to be *no part* of CHRIST's *Person*, and of no account in *Mr. Irving's* view. Whereas, on pa. 442, he makes the same sinful Humanity of CHRIST to be *every thing*—for he declares that it was the *Human* Nature only that suffered, and *that* " only according to the measure of a *Man*"—" of a *holy* Man"—which brings the matter to this conclusion—that as *Mr. Irving* maintains there was *no Sin personally* committed by CHRIST (because, as *he* would have it, the GODHEAD only was the *Person*, which, being holy, sinneth not) so there could have been no *personal Atonement*, in any shape, by way of Suffering, since *that Suffering* he declares to have been in his *Human Nature only*, which forms, in *his* esteem, *no part* of the *Person* of CHRIST. The very Premises he here lays down, in order to prove that CHRIST was not *personally* a Sinner, (though His Manhood was *fallen* Manhood and *full of Sin*) as clearly prove that He was not *personally* a *Saviour!* And from this dilemma *Mr. Irving* will never extricate himself, until he admits those two important Truths which he *denies*, viz. that the *Human* Nature *was a part* of the complex *Person* of CHRIST; (or how could He have been *complex* without it) and that His *Human* Nature also was ever *inherently* and perfectly *holy!*

---

And not only such " a very poor Wit," but " such a very barbarous Idea of GOD," too, must those " Holy Men of old" have had also, who were " moved by the HOLY GHOST" to write those " Holy Scriptures of Truth" which have been so fully quoted above in proof of the Atonement being a Satisfaction made to offended Justice by the perfect Obedience unto Death of GOD's " HOLY CHILD JESUS"—who was *ever inherently holy*—and *ever divinely righteous*.

*Mr. Irving* confesses, in pa. 147, that he is a " rebellious Man *at war* with his GOD;" and the productions of his pen which advocate the Inherent Sinfulness of the Human Nature of CHRIST, not only shew us that he is engaged in " the Siege" he speaks of in pa. 154, that " fearful Siege which is at present carried on against the very Citadel of GOD's own *Holy Being*"—but that he has assumed to himself no meaner rank than Commander in Chief of the forces he has stirred up to the Battle, to *attack* the Truth which he calls *Error*—to *expose* it, *to root it out*—to *destroy* it—and to let the last Breath be a *Testimony against* it! How then is *Mr. Irving*, as " a man at war with God," to obtain reconciliation with GOD, if the Atonement of CHRIST had no respect to

There is another Thought that I must mention here, because it involves some important Consequences which I believe *Mr. Irving* denies—namely, that his Doctrine of the " Sinfulness of the Human Nature of the LORD JESUS CHRIST" necessarily makes HIM to be chargeable with *Original Sin !* If we enquire *how* it was that CHRIST's Human Nature could be sinful, *Mr. Irving* would, I presume, reply in the very expressions he has used on pa. 424, viz. by assuming " Woman's Flesh," and thereby possessing " all the Properties of a sinful Woman's Substance." Now, not to say any thing here of that which was " born of the Virgin" being so miraculously conceived, &c. " of the HOLY GHOST"—declared to be a "new Thing"—" a holy Thing"—and that according to the Power of *Him,* " who worketh all things after the counsel of His own Will," and to whom " all things are possible ;" I observe, that if CHRIST thus took sinful Substance of the Virgin, as *her Flesh was* in the loins of *Adam* when he sinned, so *His* Flesh must have been ; and *He* thereby became just as much chargeable with Original Sin as *she* was, or any others of the fallen Posterity of *Adam* could have been : for *Mr. Irving* will have it, that the Flesh of CHRIST is only to be spoken of as *all other Flesh is,* (although no other was ever conceived and brought forth like His,) namely, " of the *same Lump as David's, Abraham's,* and *Adam's,*"—even "that sinful, corruptible, fleeting thing, of which it is said, " All Flesh is Grass"—

any bearing on the GODHEAD ? CHRIST is said to have " made *Peace* by the Blood of His Cross." The *Church* is said to have been " reconciled to GOD by the death of His Son"—and GOD Himself to have been *" pacified"* towards her ; as it is written, " And in that day thou shalt say, O LORD, I will praise thee ; though thou wast angry with me, thine anger is turned away, and thou comfortedst me," (*Isa.* xii. 1.) " That thou mayest remember, and be confounded, and never open thy mouth any more, because of thy shame, when I am *pacified* toward thee, for all that thou hast done, saith the LORD GOD." (*Ezek.* xvi. 63.) Of which *Pacification* of the *Divine Anger,* no one can have any real knowledge or experience who denies the *existence* of such Anger ; and who tells us that " the Atonement has no bearing upon the GODHEAD, but upon the *Sinner.*" *Mr. Irving* may profess " from his heart to *pity* those who, he says, are wrapped up in the *poisonous garment* of the *popular Theology,* that GOD loveth suffering, and will have it out of some one or other without any abatement," (102.) but if " some other able and as willing" hath not paid for him " the rigid Satisfaction Death for Death," good were it for him that he had never been born !

and " in it dwelleth no good thing"—but that " every variety of
Human Wickedness was inherent in it"—that "there is but
*one Human Nature;* which is not mine, thine, nor His, but
the *common unity* of our Being"—(442). And that, when
*Human Nature* was sentenced *in* the *Person* of *Adam* to
death, it was *all* sentenced, *every Particle of it whatever*"—
and that Christ "died by virtue of the common Property
of Flesh to die." Of course, Christ's Human Nature must
be included in those words " every Particle whatever"—yea,
they seem to be expressly used by *Mr. Irving* with an eye
to Christ, in order that *His* Humanity should not be excluded; and this is put beyond all doubt, by his declaring
elsewhere that the Human Nature of the Son of God" was
*actually accursed in* the *Loins* of our first Parents! Then,
it is evident, *Mr. Irving* makes Christ to have been *in*
*Adam;* and *Adam* to have been the *Head* of Christ. And
as the Scriptures assure us " All in *Adam* die," so Christ
must have *died* in *Adam*—and as by the Offence of that one
Man, *Adam, many* were *made Sinners*—even so Christ
must have been *made a Sinner,* just as much as all others in
*Adam*—there being *"no difference,"* Mr. *Irving* says, "in
alienation and guiltiness between them." And yet, though
thus in *Adam's* loins, "fallen," " sinful," and " corrupt," in
common with all mankind—" of the same Lump"—" of the
same common Nature or unity of Being" with them—with
them "accursed of God" *in* the same common Head, and
for the same Sin; and sentenced to Death as all others were
—and dying as all others did, because Christ's Flesh was
possessed of " the same common Property of Flesh to die" as
all others had, and which they possessed through *Adam's*
Sin—in the face of all these things *Mr. Irving* pretends, that
Christ avoids the charge of *Original* Sin, because he says
His Godhead *only* was His *Person,*—and His Godhead
not sinning, that Christ did not Sin—because Sin, he says,
is the Act of the *Person* rather than of *a Nature* which the
Person assumed; and Christ's *Person,* as before stated, he
there wishes to make appear, was his *Divine* Nature only.
Here, again, we find *Mr. Irving* denying in one place what, in
express words he maintains in another—namely, that the *Person* of Christ includes both His Natures, the Human and the
Divine—and in such denial he destroys the whole *Righteous-*

*ness* of the Church, since *that* was wrought out by the very Nature which *Mr. Irving* excludes from all personality in the matter of Original Sin; and which, by the same Rule, must necessarily be excluded also from all personality in the great matter of a justifying Righteousness—for, as *Mr. Irving* argues, CHRIST was not a Sinner originally because His GODHEAD did *not sin* in Adam's sinning, (although he affirms that CHRIST's *Human Nature* was " accursed *for* Sin in *Adam's* loins") so must it be maintained that no Sinner can be made personally Righteous, because it was not the GODHEAD (*Mr. Irving's Person*) of CHRIST that *obeyed* and *suffered,* but the Manhood in union with it :—and which Manhood, moreover, *Mr. Irving* declares to have been " fallen," " sinful," and " corrupt" " to the last." Thus, in attempting to put asunder what GOD has joined together, (namely, the two Natures in CHRIST's Complex Person,) and making His GODHEAD *only* to constitute His *Person* (which *Mr. Irving* here does in order to avoid the charge of Original Sin) he excludes the *Manhood* from *all personality* and from *all responsibility,* and at once deprives the Church of *all Righteousness,* and every *truly* awakened Sinner of *all* true scriptural *ground of Hope!*

It is not for *me,* my honourable Friend, to sit in final judgment upon the state of another man's Servant—" to his own Master he stands or falls"—nor is it for *me* to pretend to foretell, as by the Spirit of Prophecy, what may befall such an one in another day—yet, I cannot help viewing *Mr. Irving* as a Vessel that is launched upon a tremendous sea, with an extensive sail set, beating about upon the billows under the influence of a heavy gale. And, as such Vessel could not remain long in so dangerous a condition, so *I* conceive *Mr. Irving* cannot long continue in his present sentiments, under his present circumstances; and that *if* he ever *really knew any thing* of " the Truth as it is in JESUS," by *divine* Teaching, (for, how the " *Spirit* of Truth" can really dwell in one who speaks such Things, and with such Enmity against the Truth, as *Mr. Irving* does, may well demand the doubt,) the LORD will be pleased of His great Mercy to grant him " Repentance unto Life for those awful Errors he now maintains, and which assuredly lead to Death"—or, that we shall, ere long, find *his* name enrolled amongst the avowed

*Arians* or *Socinians* of the day—or that he will fall in some other way.* And then will such of the LORD's Children as may have been entangled, (as may have been "bewitched," or fascinated, as the Apostle says, in *Gal.* iii. 1.) with *Mr. Irving's* Reasonings, wonder at themselves, that *they* should ever have indulged for a moment *the most distant Hope* of Salvation *from* Sin, through one who was declared to have been just as *inherently Wicked* as themselves—or have formed the least expectation of deliverance *from* the *Curse* of the *Law* through one who was Himself declared to have been "*accursed* in the Loins of *Adam*" just as much as themselves—and who *died*, not because of any *Suretyship* engagement on account of His People, but because it was the "*common Pro-*

---

* Should any one accuse the Author of the above Remarks with being either *personal* or *uncharitable*, he would screen himself from the *first* Accusation beneath those words of *Mr. Irving*, in pa. 422 of No. 3 of " *The Morning Watch;*" where he speaks of " the *Coles* and the *Haldanes*," as " Sectaries and Schismatics, who are to him as Heathen Men and Publicans !" And from the *second* he would take shelter beneath the following quotations from " The Orthodox and Catholic Doctrine of our LORD's Human Nature," pa. 142, and Preface x. " They call this *personality*. I deny it ; it is the opposite. It is not the *Persons*, but their *Opinions*, their *Errors*, their *destructive* and *seductive* ERRORS we are set against. *This* is *Love* to the *Person*. Thus I will carry myself with *forbearance* to the *Men*, but with *unsparing destructiveness* to their *erroneous Doctrines*." " *I defy them* to produce out of *my* Writings *one Word* of *uncharitableness* towards the Persons of any one." [See also the preceding Note on pa. 53 of this Letter.]

If, therefore, *Mr. Irving* be not chargeable with the smallest possible taint of *uncharitableness*, in declaring of his Opponents, as he does, that they are " *his* Enemies," (*Pref.* xii.) and " the Enemies of the *Truth*," (114,) that they are an " Ignorant Multitude, whom blind Guides are deceiving to their own destruction,"(23)—" Idle Ones," and "Empty Ones," " Railers and Fools"— " Fiery and furious Schismatics, whom *Satan* hath set on to resist and pervert the Truth." " Evangelicals driving full tilt to Error," 141. " Sectaries who are already drowned in it," 141. " Those Hordes of Sectaries (and unlearned Churchmen) who proclaim that it is a Heresy to say that JESUS CHRIST took *Sinful* Flesh," 21. Men who are " wrapped up in the poisonous Garment of the Popular Theology," 102. " Men to whom " GOD hath *sent strong Delusion*, that they should *believe* a *Lie*," 23. " Malicious Men ! Wicked Railers ! who will not learn Charity and Love." " His Enemies, who *shall* flounder on in *Error*, and never come to see or love the Truth, until they learn to walk by the same Rule of Love," (*Pref.* xii.) If all these assertions, and multiplied more of a similar sort that are selected in the long catalogue given in the Note on pa. 53, subject *Mr. Irving* to no charge of *uncharitableness* on that account, the Author of the above Letter, and of these Notes, can have nothing to fear from any of the Accusations that may be brought against him by *Mr. Irving*, or by any of his Friends, either on the score of personality, or of uncharitableness.

*perty* of His Flesh to die," and therefore His *common Flesh* shared the *common Fate* of *all common Men*, in and through one common Parent, *Adam!*—And who *could not* possibly have obeyed the Law for His People, being *Himself inherently sinful*—and who actually *did not* (for aught that appears in *Mr. Irving's* statements) since the GODHEAD *only* is made by *Mr. Irving* to be CHRIST'S PERSON, and the GODHEAD could not yield any Obedience to the Law under which the *Creature* was made, any more than it could suffer, bleed, or die, for the Creature's Sin !

Permit me then, my honourable and highly honoured Friend, before I close this long Epistle, most faithfully, most respectfully, and in the very spirit of Christian Love, most earnestly

---

The sacred Word of GOD, " unto which we do well to take heed, as unto a Light that shineth in a dark place," exhorts us to " prove all Things," and " to hold fast those things which are good ;" to bring all " to the Law and to the Testimony ;" to " try the Spirits" also, " whether they are of God." And while it affords us certain rules by which we are to form our judgment of " the *Children* of GOD and the Children of the *Devil*," we are not left without Witness by which those *Servants* of the LORD, whom *He* is pleased to *send* into His Vineyard " to feed the Church of GOD which He has purchased with His own Blood," are to be known from those who, like *Ahimaaz* of old, " run without being sent ;" to whom the " Captain of the LORD's Host" gives neither Commission nor Tidings, although they are permitted thus to run for their own Reproof and Correction, if not for the Instruction of others also.

The faithful Servants of the LORD, whom he is pleased to make the Stewards of the Mysteries of the Kingdom of Heaven, have " a necessity laid upon" them by which they are constrained to " Cry aloud, and spare not, but to lift up their Voices like Trumpets," against the Errors and the Sins of the professing people of GOD ; but if *this* ERROR is not to be opposed at the very point of the Sword of Truth, for fear of the charge of being " *personal ;*" or *that* SIN is not to be met by the holy Arm of the divine Law, lest we should incur the blame of being " uncharitable"— Error and Sin would not only stalk abroad unmolested, but Truth and Holiness would be constrained to hide their heads in the secret corners, as if they only, and they always were deserving of the shade. For who that maintains erroneous Sentiments, and especially such delusive and deadly ones as *Mr. Irving's*, will like to have them opposed, so *faithfully* opposed as they ought to be, and must be, by those who know such Errors to be no better than " *Lies*," in which such erroneous Teachers or Hearers have taken refuge ; and " *Falsehood*," under which they have hid themselves. (*Isa.* xxviii. 15.) But, blessed be GOD, " Great is the Truth, and it must prevail !" working as it doth its own Triumphs by its own Energies. For,

" TRUTH like an Arrow from JEHOVAH's Bow,
Conviction on its barbed point conveys,
Swift to the Heart of each rebellious Foe,
And cuts a passage for JEHOVAH's praise."　　　SWAINE.

to warn and to admonish you against the Errors here complained of, as I would my own Soul, (and that too, in the very Language of the Patriarch of old,) "O my Soul! come not thou into this *(Mr. Irving's)* Secret : unto their Assembly mine Honour be not thou united;" for "Destruction and Misery are in this way," and "the way of peace" it is not! "There is a way which seemeth right unto a man, but the end thereof is the way of death." Let me intreat you not to reject this Communication on a first perusal, because it opposes the Sentiments you may have already too favourably received; or because it repeats so often the very expressions opposed; but imitate the good King *Hezekiah* when he had received the Letter from *Sennacherib*, by spreading it before the LORD; and may the SPIRIT of *Hezekiah's* GOD, as "the

---

It is not instructive Truth, but "seductive and destructive Error," that the Author of these pages has opposed ; which, in the Word of GOD we are exhorted to "cease from hearing," (*Prov.* xix. 27.) and from which "to turn away." In so doing he has endeavoured to carry himself, (in *Mr. Irving's* own Language) "with *forbearance* to the Men, but with *unsparing destructiveness* to their *erroneous Doctrines*," (142.) And in this spirit, "with the greatest plainness of Speech and the most unflinching Faithfulness, he hesitates not to proclaim that *Mr. Irving's Foundation* is—ROTTENNESS, and his *Superstructure*—STUBBLE! That "the line of *Confusion* is stretched out upon it, and the stones of *Emptiness:*" and that the HOLY ONE of Israel will assuredly visit it "with everlasting Destruction from the presence of the LORD, and from the Glory of His Power," seeing that the *Foundation* thereof is laid in the avowed *inherent* WICKEDNESS of the *Human Nature* of the LORD JESUS CHRIST, and the *Superstructure* set up in the *unchanged* SINFULNESS thereof!!!

"But *what* a System of Theology is *that*" (to use *Mr. Irving's* own Words) whose BASE is *very* WICKEDNESS—the avowed *inherent* WICKEDNESS, of THAT which was *begotten* by the SPIRIT of ALL HOLINESS, and is declared to be "*That* HOLY THING," by the SPIRIT of ALL TRUTH? Such *inherent* WICKEDNESS, or *unchanged Sinfulness* also running throughout the *whole* SUPERSTRUCTURE, "From the Foundation to the Dome!" In *Mr. Irving's* own Words I will put the Reply : "Oh, it is a *most strange* DELUSION! it is a STRONG *Delusion*," (120.) "A *wild* HYPOTHESIS and *most fearful* ERROR," (110.) "A *pestilent* HERESY, which coming in will root out *Atonement, Redemption, Regeneration*, the Work of the SPIRIT, and the *Human Nature* of CHRIST altogether," (54.) "A *destructive* FALSEHOOD, by the ingenuity and the perversity of Men fabricated out of Truth," (117.) "The *Devil's* LIE, which cannot be *held*, nor *borne with*, save at the *great risk* and *peril* to immortal Souls," (122.) "A *wretched, Soul-destroying* ERROR," (153.) "A *Vile* and *abominable* Fiction," (154.) "A *Doctrine* that is DAMNABLE : that to *believe* it is to *believe* a LIE : to *die* in the *Faith* of it is to *die* in *the Faith* of a LIE : and which like every Lie will work the *Glory* of the *Devil*, who was a Liar from the beginning, and not the glory of JESUS CHRIST, who is THE TRUTH."

*Orthodox Doctrine,* pa. 141.

Spirit of Wisdom and of Revelation in the Knowledge of the Lord Jesus," lead you also to discern, in answer to Prayer, with whom the Truth lies; for, between *Mr. Irving's* views and *mine* on the subjects in question, there is no smaller difference than between Error and Truth—Darkness and Light —Sin and Holiness—Death and Life—eternal Misery and everlasting Felicity!

And now would "I commend you to God, and to the Word of His Grace, which is able to build you up, and give you an Inheritance among all them that are sanctified through Faith which is in Christ Jesus." May you indeed learn, by *believing*, what you cannot believe through mere Reason or human Learning; since Revelation's Mysteries are understood by believing, rather than believed by reasoning on them. *This* Belief is the gift of God: and it is the nature of divine Faith to believe God upon His *bare Word;* and that *against* Sense, in things *invisible;* and *against* Reason in things *incredible;* for, while *Sense* corrects *Imagination, Reason* corrects *Sense,* but Faith *corrects* both! And may " He who is able to keep you from falling, and to present you faultless before the Throne of His Glory with exceeding joy," be with you, my Honoured Friend, and with yours,

Is the sincere desire, and earnest prayer, of

Your very obedient Servant,

For the Lord's sake,

*The Mount,*
FARNINGHAM,
*Dec. 21, 1829.*

W. H. C.

*⁎* The Postscript, referred to in some of the preceding Notes, is intended to appear at the Author's earliest leisure.

*E. JUSTINS and SON, Printers, Brick Lane, Spitalfields.*

www.ingramcontent.com/pod-product-compliance
Lightning Source LLC
LaVergne TN
LVHW061219060426
835508LV00014B/1356